Understanding the Steiner Waldorf Approach

Understanding the Steiner Waldorf Approach is a much-needed source of information for those wishing to extend and consolidate their under-standing of the Steiner Waldorf approach. It will enable the reader to analyse the essential elements of the Steiner Waldorf approach to early childhood and its relationship to quality early years practice.

Exploring all areas of the curriculum, including observation and assess-ment, child development, play, repetition and the environment, this book:

- describes the key principles of the Steiner Waldorf approach to early childhood with examples from Steiner settings;
- provides students and practitioners with the relevant information about a key pedagogical influence on high-quality early years practice in the UK;
- highlights the key ideas that practitioners should consider when reviewing and reflecting on their own practice;
- can be used as the basis for continuing professional development and action research.

Written to support the work of all those in the field of early years education and childcare, this is a vital text for students, early years and childcare practitioners, teachers, early years professionals, children's centre professionals, lecturers, advisory teachers, head teachers and setting managers.

Janni Nicol has worked as a Steiner kindergarten teacher in South Africa and the UK. She is now the UK early childhood representative for Steiner Waldorf schools and kindergartens and writes, consults and lectures on Steiner early childhood in the UK and internationally.

Jill Tina Taplin works in teacher education in the UK and internationally, advising, teaching and writing, after many years as a Steiner kinder-garten teacher in Scotland and England.

Understanding the . . . Approach
Series Editors: Pat Brunton and Linda Thornton

This new series provides a much-needed source of information for those wishing to extend and consolidate their understanding of international approaches to early years education and childcare. The books will enable the reader to analyse the essential elements of each approach and its relationship to quality early years practice.

Each book:

- describes the key principles of the approach to early childhood with practical examples and case studies;
- provides students and practitioners with the relevant information about a key pedagogical influence on high-quality early years practice;
- highlights the key ideas that practitioners should consider when reviewing and reflecting on their own practice;
- can be used as the basis for continuing professional development and action research.

Written to support the work of all those in the field of early years education and childcare, these will be invaluable texts for students, early years and childcare practitioners, teachers, early years professionals, children's centre professionals, lecturers, advisory teachers, head teachers and setting managers.

Understanding the Steiner Waldorf Approach

Early years education in practice

Janni Nicol and Jill Tina Taplin

Routledge
Taylor & Francis Group

LONDON AND NEW YORK

First published 2012
by Routledge
2 Park Square, Milton Park, Abingdon, Oxon OX14 4RN

Simultaneously published in the USA and Canada
by Routledge
711 Third Avenue, New York, NY 10017

Routledge is an imprint of the Taylor & Francis Group, an informa business

British Library Cataloguing in Publication Data
A catalogue record for this book is available from the British Library

Library of Congress Cataloging in Publication Data
Nicol, Janni.
    Understanding the Steiner Waldorf approach : early years education in practice / Janni Nicol and Jill Taplin.
        p. cm.
    1. Early childhood education--Great Britain. 2. Waldorf method of education—Great Britain. I. Taplin, Jill. II. Title.
    LB1139.3.G7.N55 2011
    372.210942—dc23   2011036762

ISBN: 978–0–415–59715–9 (hbk)
ISBN: 978–0–415–59716–6 (pbk)
ISBN: 978–0–203–18146–1 (ebk)

Typeset in Palatino and Futura
by Keystroke, Station Road, Codsall, Wolverhampton

Printed and bound in Great Britain by
TJ International Ltd, Padstow, Cornwall

Contents

Acknowledgements

We would like to offer our thanks to those known and unknown contributors, to our colleagues, friends and families and to those kindergarten teachers who continue to be role models worthy of imitation. All photos have been provided by the *Kindling (Journal for Steiner Waldorf Early Childhood)* archive.

Introduction

Rudolf Steiner (1861–1925), in his many lectures and writings, pointed to the need for a spiritual renewal of Western culture, in areas including agriculture, economics, the sciences, religion and the arts, as well as in education, as discussed further in this book. Today there are thousands of schools, farms, clinics and other organisations doing practical work based on his insights. He offered a comprehensive path of spiritual development and research, which he said could contribute to the creation of a more humane world.

For nearly 100 years the unique and unusual education he founded has spread and grown throughout the world. The educational philosophy, which was developed in the first Waldorf School in 1919, was based on the thoughts, ideas and spiritual insights which Steiner gave of the developing human being. Waldorf education is also known as Steiner or Steiner Waldorf education and encompasses the child from pre-birth throughout life. In many countries, particularly in Europe, the day care, kindergartens and schools are fully state funded, and the later school starting date of many countries fits with the later introduction of formal learning which Steiner propounded.

The aim of the approach is to help the child to develop into a morally responsible, free individual, able to fulfil his or her unique destiny. To do this, the focus is on following and extending Steiner's ideas on the nature of childhood and the development of the growing human being, which, for education purposes in particular, is divided into seven-year periods.

For the first seven years (the years of early childhood), education is taken up with the nurturing of a strong healthy physical body, out of imitation of the practitioner (or kindergarten teacher) in an enabling 'home like' environment. This takes place in a pleasant and calm setting, which, in the case of kindergartens, focuses on developing practical life skills in mixed age (familial) surroundings. The use of the term 'kinder-garten' to refer to a class of children aged between three and six or seven years old, is common in Steiner Waldorf terminology and will be used in this book. This book focuses on the stage of development from birth to age seven, giving examples of how Steiner's ideas are put into practice.

Many who hear about the education are keen to visit a setting, and it is difficult for the kindergarten teachers who are trying to create this inti-mate and sensorially protective environment to accommodate visitors. (However, schools and settings regularly hold open days and informa-tion sessions for interested visitors as well as fund-raising events such as summer fairs and Christmas markets, which do convey something of the flavour of the education.) It is very difficult to give a true picture in writing of what visitors experience when they are in the kindergarten as it appeals to what Steiner refers to as the 'feeling life' – it impacts emo-tionally, and visitors have described their experiences as 'it took me back to my own childhood', 'it made me want to cry' (some do); 'I felt like a little child again', 'I felt comforted' and so on. It is difficult to intellec-tually understand the emotional impact the experience has on the indi-vidual but we hope that the liberal use of examples, anecdotes and descriptions in the following chapters will help.

Often there are comparisons made between the Montessori, Reggio and Steiner approaches, but, as you will see in this book, although some of the impulses are similar the philosophy underpinning the principles and much of the practice is fundamentally different and distinct. Rod Parker-Rees, in his introduction to *Meeting the Child in Steiner Kindergartens: An exploration of beliefs, values and practices* said, 'Where the Reggio Emilia preschools appear to buzz with the energy of children busily engaged in studying all aspects of their world, Steiner kindergartens are more likely to impress visitors with a pervasive feeling of calm, unhurried "just being" – more like a home than a studio or academy' (Parker-Rees 2011: 6)

Many educators who have been touched by some aspect of their experience in a kindergarten would like to adopt the Steiner Waldorf approach, or parts of it. There are some aspects that are transferable; however, as you will see from this book, the philosophy is one that calls for immersion in Steiner's insights and theories of child development. It also calls for self-development and transformative learning on the part of the educator. It was Froebel's belief that early-years teachers should ideally be like a 'mother made conscious' (Steedman 1985), it was Steiner's that they should develop themselves in order to be a role model worth of imitation in thought, word and deed.

Background to the UK interest in the Steiner Waldorf approach

As you will read in Chapter 1, interest in the UK began with the visit to the UK by Rudolf Steiner in 1923. The approach was developed by the teachers involved in the first kindergartens, and much of the practice came from studying Steiner's ideas on the developing child and Steiner's other impulses. These are explained in more detail in subsequent chapters. Many readers will find similarities in other approaches, such as in Montessori, with the spiritual view of the child and the self-development and transformative learning of the educator. Froebel has contributed much to the approach, in the ring time, in the household activities and the outdoors as a classroom which is also a feature of the recent forest schools movement. The creativity has much in common with the Reggio approach, and many Steiner educators contributed to the One Hundred Languages exhibition in Cambridge in 1997, particularly in the areas of storytelling, puppetry and play. It was after this exhibition that interest in visiting kindergartens began in earnest. Local authorities began asking Steiner practitioners to give workshops, and universities began including Steiner early childhood in their comparative-education modules. Steiner practitioners were consulted during the initial Foundation Stage framework planning. The Steiner and Montessori educational approaches are recognised in the UK as having their own ethos and curriculum, distinctly different from all others. (See Appendix I.)

In the review of the early years foundation stage (EYFS) in 2011, Dame Clare Tickell said,

> Ministers have consistently agreed that there is a conflict between the philosophy of these [Steiner] settings and some of the early learning goals, and have granted exemptions from the affected goals to this end. *I recommend that the Government extend the exemptions from these early learning goals to all settings within the Steiner-Waldorf (Schools Fellowship).*

The structure of the chapters

At the beginning of each chapter there is a brief summary of the content, followed by a more detailed description of the aspect under consideration. References relating to each chapter are included at the end of the chapter. Each chapter is summarised in a set of ten key points. Finally, there is a section entitled 'Reflections on the Steiner Waldorf Approach'. It is offered as a starting point, not a comprehensive list. It is primarily designed to be used as a group exercise, to highlight issues you may wish to consider as a team when reflecting on your practice and reflects questions that we have often been asked over the years when introducing Steiner Waldorf early-childhood education.

The structure of the book

A glossary is included at the end of this introduction to introduce some of the terms used, and at the end of the book there is a list of key texts to encourage readers to extend their own research and understanding of the Steiner Waldorf approach.

Chapter 1 describes the history and personal background of Rudolf Steiner, his original work in many areas and how he developed his ideas on an educational approach that met the needs of the 'whole' human being. It also presents the beginnings of Steiner Waldorf early childhood education and how it grew to be an international movement. In Chapter 2, the twelve essential principles of Steiner Waldorf early childhood are discussed. The image of the child as a spiritual being, bringing gifts and with particular tasks to do in his or her lifetime is introduced. This stands behind the educator's reverence for the child and sense of responsibility as an educator to be involved in a continuous process of inner self-development. Chapter 3 focuses on the picture of child development that underpins Steiner Waldorf practice. Steiner's ideas of both the threefold and the fourfold human being are introduced, and the division of education into seven-year stages is explained. Then the methodology is outlined that springs from the focus of the first seven years as those of imitation and example. Chapter 4 begins to look more closely at this methodology and leads into the heart of the Steiner Waldorf setting by describing the environment where the child's senses are protected and authentic learning can take place. All the children's areas, indoors and out, are designed to be both beautiful and functional as the environment enables the practitioners to bring the simple activities of everyday life to the children within a 'home from home' atmosphere. In Chapter 5, the practitioner's use of young children's innate imitative capacities as the prime teaching method is explored. The Steiner practitioner sees both the environment and the activity of the adults as actually forming the children in ways that will affect them for the rest of their lives. The development of imitative skills in the growing child is discussed as is the importance of the models given by the older children in a mixed-age kindergarten. Chapter 6 reviews the child's self-initiated play in early-childhood education and its central place in the Steiner setting. Steiner pedagogy sees this kind of play as the young child's way of exploring and developing his or her own learning needs, and practitioners provide time and space in the ideal environment and sensitively support such play. In Chapter 7, the key concepts of rhythm and repetition in the Steiner setting are covered. We explain how these concepts support early-childhood learning and build confidence and resilience in the child. Details are given of how the Steiner setting works with rhythm through the day, the week and the year in a way that engenders a mood of unselfconscious participation in the children. Chapter 8 looks at domestic and artistic activities in the Steiner early-childhood setting. The pedagogical significance of domestic activities, or the art of living, is described, as is the value of time spent in artistic creativity for both the child and for the adult who works as an educator or carer. Examples are included of the activities common in Steiner kindergartens. Chapter 9 looks at child observation and its development within Steiner pedagogy into the child study – a spiritual and artistic deed undertaken by a group of colleagues. Record-keeping and the making of both formative and summative assessments for individual children are also addressed. Chapter 10 brings us to the sense of colleagueship that needs to be built in the adults around the child, including not only parents[1] and practitioners but also support staff and specialists. From the initial meeting with the family to the family's ongoing part in the life of the setting, the child is nurtured and supported by close partnership. Working with outside agencies and Steiner-trained specialists is also covered here. Chapter 11 ranges through current issues of interest in Steiner pedagogy. These include work with the very young child in day-care settings and parent and child groups, home childcare and home schooling, wrap-around care and working with the mixed-age kindergarten, with particular emphasis on the needs of the oldest children. The attitude of Steiner pedagogy towards early formal learning and electronic technology is discussed as is working with diversity and inclusion in the Steiner setting.

Appendix 1 considers future issues, including initiatives and challenges to Steiner early-childhood education in Britain and worldwide. Brief introductions are given to the organisations both at home and abroad that support Steiner education and Steiner teacher education. Appendix II lists typical equipment and activities that are to be found in the Steiner Waldorf setting, as discussed in Chapters 4 and 8. An example of a seasonal 'ring time' is given in Appendix III to illustrate the descriptions of ring time that are in Chapters 5 and 7. Appendix IV provides an example of a child-observation schema as discussed in Chapter 9.

Note

1 *'Parents' could mean mothers, fathers and carers.*

References

Parker-Rees, R. (2011) 'Introduction: Ways of Knowing Children', in R. Parker-Rees (ed.), *Meeting the Child in Steiner Kindergartens: An Exploration of Beliefs, Values and Practices*, London: Routledge, pp. 1–12.
Steedman, J. (1985) 'The Mother Made Conscious': The Historical Development of a Primary School Pedagogy'. *History Workshop Journal*, 20(1): 148–9.
Tickell, C. (2011) *The Early Years: Foundations for Life, Health and Learning – An Independent Report on the Early Years Foundation Stage to Her Majesty's Government*, available online at http://www.education.gov.uk/tickellreview. (Accessed 30/3/2011)

The authors

Janni Nicol and Jill Tina Taplin have been practising kindergarten teachers for many years, both having been pioneer teachers in kindergartens which have developed into full Steiner schools. Their understanding of the Steiner Waldorf approach is based in practical life work and deep study of Rudolf Steiner's ideas, both in theory and practice. They have worked as kindergarten teacher trainers and as advisers, visiting many kindergartens in the UK and around the world. The picture of the education given in this book is both theoretical and practical, and they have tried to focus on those areas that address the principles underpinning the practice.

Glossary

educator   As referred to in the book, 'educator' could mean kindergarten teacher, assistant, or parent or carer: anyone who is in contact with the child. There is acknowledgement that the parent is the child's first and primary educator.

kindergarten   'kindergarten' was the name originally used by Friedrich Wilhelm August Fröbel to describe his pre-school setting, referred to by him as a 'paradise garden'. In German it is a directly translated as 'children's garden' or 'a garden for children'. In this book, we have used many terms to describe the Steiner Waldorf setting or early childhood setting. 'Setting' is commonly used in the UK to describe the place where children are cared for and educated in or out of the home. 'Kindergarten' is how most Steiner settings refer to themselves, and is how they are registered with the Steiner Waldorf Schools Fellowship (SWSF). A kindergarten is generally for the ages from three to seven years and runs in the mornings only. Aftercare is often provided as extended kindergarten, but it is not a repeat of the morning session. Some Steiner Waldorf early-childhood provisions have playgroup or nursery classes which are for the two- to four-year-olds, but in others these younger children are included in the mixed-age kindergartens. Parent-and-child groups are for parents and carers who accompany their young babies and toddlers to a specific Steiner group run by a professional leader. Daycare covers a wider age range than kindergarten, usually includes babies and toddlers and could run for extended hours. 'Centre' could describe a setting where more than one activity takes place, and a Steiner Waldorf early-childhood centre generally includes playgroup, parent-and-child group, kindergarten and aftercare. Many are attached to Steiner schools which provide the full age range of primary and in some cases secondary education. 'Setting' could also be used to describe the place where home childcare (childminding) takes place, possibly for a wider age range.

kindergarten teacher and assistant   In this book we have used many terms to describe the Steiner Waldorf kindergarten teacher. 'Kindergarten teacher' is the most commonly used term, but 'kindergarten practitioner' helps to emphasise how distinct this is from the normal role of a teacher. In the UK, we also refer to the Steiner practitioner or early childhood teacher or leader. In the USA the term used is often 'educarer. Kindergarten teachers are male or female, and there are practising male kindergarten teachers in the UK. The kindergarten teacher is also the registered person, the leader, the manager and the key person. The kindergarten assistant is in place to support the teacher in the kindergarten. He or she may be a student undertaking a work placement as part of training. Most kindergartens are of such a size that a teacher plus one assistant fulfil the statutory requirements for adult-to-child ratio, but in the case of larger groups additional assistants will be present to meet the required ratios.

Steiner Waldorf The names used to describe the education are used differently in many countries. In some it is 'Waldorf' (referring to the original name given to the Stuttgart school started by Emil Molt for the workers of his Waldorf Astoria cigarette factory) or 'Steiner', after Rudolf Steiner. In some countries, both names are used. There are times when the content of the education is referred to as 'Waldorf', as in 'the Waldorf curriculum' or 'Waldorf education'. In this book we have used all three forms: 'Steiner', 'Waldorf' and 'Steiner Waldorf'.

1 History and foundations

Introduction

In this chapter we will look at the history and personal background of Rudolf Steiner (see Fig. 1.1) and how he developed his ideas on an educational approach meeting the needs of the 'whole' human being.

Rudolf Steiner and his work

During the late 1800s and early in the 1900s there were great changes happening in Europe: the beginning of the Industrial Revolution brought about the first electric light, travelling took place by car and airplane, cinema, telephone and telegraph changed the way people communicated with each other, travellers were able to publish photographs of their journeys, and scientists focused their attention on movement, matter and overcoming the forces of nature. This was the beginning of the 'modern (materialist) age' when mankind no longer separated science and religion, knowledge and faith, matter and spirit – all these things were now open for discussion, and 'free thinkers' developed who took these discussions into different dimensions: Einstein, Darwin, Tolstoy, Marx, Freud. The world was full of intellectuals, artists, dramatists, thinkers, politicians, scientists and explorers. It was an exciting time in which to be born.

Rudolf Joseph Lorenz Steiner was born to Franziska Blie and Johann Steiner on 27 February 1861. He was their oldest child, followed by a brother and a sister. His father was a hunter, working in the service of a count, in Lower Austria north of the Danube (now Croatia). The Count refused to give permission to Rudolf's parents to marry, so Johann left his

Figure 1.1 Rudolf Steiner.

employment and joined the railways as a telegraph operator. He was sent to Kraljevic (Croatia), where Rudolf was born. The children took part in family life, sharing household chores and working in the orchard or with the pigs. Rudolf was fascinated by his father's telegraph, and also by nature, and spent time with farm workers and woodcutters, collecting berries and fruit. He preferred to be on his own and was an independent and isolated child, particularly because of some early clairvoyant experiences he had (which he described in his memoirs) and also because he had no time to play with other children. He had few toys but often referred to picture books with figures that could be made to move by pulling strings attached to them at the bottom. He associated little stories with these figures, 'to whom one gave a part of their life by pulling the strings. Many a time have I sat by the hour poring over the picture-books with my sister. Besides, I learned from them by myself the first steps in reading' (Steiner 1928: 7). He spent a lot of time with his father and learned to write by imitating him. He was as interested in the shapes of the letters as in putting them together.

At the small village school which Rudolf attended at around eight years of age, he first learned to read, and from that moment he devoured books on all kinds of subjects. He studied the people around him, the mysteries of the Mass, the social tension between the aristocracy and the workers, the industrial activities of the factories and railways and the peace and beauty of nature. He also discovered geometry, which he said gave him happiness for the first time. He realised that knowledge of the world could be carried within and that one could speak of the world of the mind with clarity and scientific precision.

At secondary school, Steiner studied mathematics, science and philosophy. He taught himself Greek, Latin and accountancy and gave lessons to private pupils to supplement his income. At the age of eighteen he went to university in Vienna, where he studied biology, chemistry, physics and mathematics and attended classes in philosophy and literature. He continued studying everything that interested him, including his experiences of the spiritual world through clairvoyant incidents. He became determined to find a way to explain his spiritual experiences in the light of scientific materialistic concepts of the time in which he lived. Steiner was asked to edit the complete works of Johann Wolfgang von Goethe, and here he began to make links between scientific knowledge and his own observations of the actions of spiritual forces.

Steiner worked as a tutor for a wealthy Viennese family, looking after their four boys, one of whom had physical and learning difficulties (who ended up becoming a medical doctor). It was through these experiences of trying to find a way to educate this child that Steiner began to develop his theories of education and of therapy. After achieving his doctorate in 1891, he developed his spiritual and scientific research and wrote his first book, *The Philosophy of Freedom*, where he described for the first time the relationships between his observation of the modern natural sciences to an inner world. He named this spiritual science 'anthroposophy' and gave countless courses and lectures throughout Europe, setting out his programme for spiritual reform of life in the areas of art, education, politics, economics, medicine, agriculture and the Christian religion. His love of drama, theatre, puppetry and music brought him onto the lecture circuit, and he wrote many journals and papers.

The education of the child

Steiner was invited by Emil Molt, the Director of the Waldorf Astoria Cigarette factory in Stuttgart, Germany, to give a series of lectures to the workers in his factory. Molt had read an essay by Steiner called 'The Education of the Child in the Light of Anthroposophy' (written in 1907) and appealed to Steiner to develop this 'art' of education so that he could open a school for the children of his factory workers. It was important to both that education should not impose ideology, whether political, religious and economic – nor an anthroposophical one either. Anthroposophy should also not be taught as a subject but used to inform teachers about the global image of man, the respect for human individuality and for self-development. It was during these lectures that Steiner developed his spiritual insights, including that of reincarnation and karma, in his ideas on the development of the individual from pre-birth to after death. He gave indications on the developmental phases of the human being, which he explained in much detail, and spoke about his ideas for social renewal after the impact of the First World War. The first group of teachers encouraged by Rudolf Steiner developed the educational approach with him. Steiner said that in order to educate teachers must educate themselves throughout their life and that only the teacher who is committed to this will be able to inspire students.

The first Waldorf school

Steiner ceremonially opened the first 'Free Waldorf School' on 7 September 1919. It was, from the beginning, a full primary and secondary school for 256 children drawn mainly from the families of the workers in the factory. They were divided into eight classes, and it was the first time that children of both sexes, from different social strata, nationalities, religions and abilities all shared a classroom. Steiner's educational reform also worked with the structure of the school management, bringing his ideas on social reform, namely the threefold structure, where governance took place in the three areas of the cultural life, economic activity and political administration.

Although Steiner was an idealist who never compromised his beliefs, he was also a pragmatist in the realm of education. He agreed with the Stuttgart educational authorities that although the Waldorf curriculum would remain uncompromised and that the students would not follow the state curriculum, the pupils would be able to transfer from the Waldorf school to state schools at certain key stages. He modified the work done in the school to ensure that the children had also covered all the subject matter and attained the same skills as children in other schools at the appropriate ages.

Steiner initiatives worldwide

Steiner gave thousands of lectures and courses throughout Europe, setting out his programme for spiritual reform of life in the areas of the arts, education, politics, economics, medicine, agriculture, religion and social organisation. He died on 30 March 1925 in Dornach, while still working on his autobiography. Notes of his lectures were published in countless papers and books and were translated into many languages. These lectures form the basis for further study, and today there are an estimated 10,000 initiatives worldwide working in the fields of:

- education (Steiner Waldorf kindergartens, schools and training centres);
- agriculture (biodynamic farms and vineyards);
- art (architecture, eurythmy, puppetry, theatre, music, sculpture, painting);

- medicine (anthroposophical clinics, hospitals, homoeopathic pharmacies, training centres for doctors and nurses, massage, art and movement therapies, beauty products);
- natural science (water purification, composting, astronomy);
- scientific research, literature, philosophy, social renewal (care of the dying, and the Camphill schools for people with special education needs);
- economics (banks and ethical investment).

The beginnings of Steiner Waldorf early-childhood education

In 1914, before the first school opened, Rudolf Steiner met Elisabeth Grünelius. Grünelius had joined a group of artists working under Steiner's direction on the building of the first Gotheanum in Dornach, Switzerland. (This is now the headquarters of the pedagogical section of Steiner Waldorf schools and other initiatives working out of the guidance given by Rudolf Steiner, such as anthroposophical medicine, biodynamic farming and the arts.) Elisabeth attended lectures by Steiner before continuing with her studies at the Pestalozzi–Froebel Seminar in Berlin, where she was studying to become a kindergarten teacher.

Steiner would have liked to include the kindergarten years (which he felt were the most important) in the first school and asked Elisabeth to write a proposal on how one would work with three to five year olds. She wrote:

> I felt I had to have experience first. One could not sit at a table and figure it all out. Today it is perhaps difficult to imagine a time when no one had worked consciously with the imitative capacities of the child. We need to remember that class teachers teach, but the kindergarten teacher must show what should be done through her life and being.
>
> (Howard 2006: 6)

In 1920, due to a change in school starting date, there were a number of pre-schoolers who needed care for a few months, and it was with this group of six-year-olds that many of the basic ideas were developed. Grünelius had only Rudolf Steiner's statements that meditation should be the basis of life in the kindergarten and that she was to work out of

imitation – two entirely radical thoughts which she had never encoun-
tered before in her training for early-childhood education! She had no
toys for the children to play with and therefore spent much of the time
outside. The children did activities such as drawing, watercolour painting and clay modelling. She told stories to the children, learning them 'by
heart'. The class did not last long due to lack of space and financial difficulties, but Elisabeth continued to extend her studies, attending Steiner's
lectures and developing her own ideas. In 1926, eighteen months after
Steiner's death, the first kindergarten finally opened. Elisabeth built up
the activities out of her own 'sense' of what the children needed, working
meditatively and with imitation rather than didactics. Susan Howard
wrote the following in her article on the beginning of the Waldorf
kindergarten movement:

> Once she invited a basket maker to come and work in the presence of the
> children. 'He was a young man, and he had his shirt sleeves rolled up so that the
> children could see how strong he was. He had a big basket, and he finished it
> with large branches. On the next day, in the cloakroom, I saw reeds hanging
> from the coat hook of one of the children, a very inhibited girl. I asked her why
> she needed the reeds. "To make baskets," she replied. Then I immediately went
> out and bought reeds and bottoms for baskets and on the next day, all the four-
> year-olds made baskets. I wanted to help them, but they could do it themselves.
> They never could have done that if they had not seen the basket maker at work.'
>
> (Howard 2006: 2)

Klara Hatterman, a young woman from Germany who wanted to
become a Waldorf kindergarten teacher, asked Elisabeth to start a kindergarten training course, but Elisabeth did not feel ready for this and said
that she needed more experience. Klara became Elisabeth's assistant for a
while, until she founded a small 'home' kindergarten near a Waldorf
school in Hanover, Germany, in 1931. The kindergartens blossomed, but
the two schools were eventually closed by the Nazis. The home kindergarten, which was less visible, remained open until 1941 when it too was
closed, as was Klara's next home kindergarten in Dresden.

Elisabeth went to the USA in 1940, where she founded two kindergartens and published her book *Early Childhood Education and the Waldorf
School Plan*, which was translated into many languages. She founded
another kindergarten in France in 1954 when she returned to Europe. In
1955, a second version of her book was published in England, *Educating
the Young Child*.

Klara opened her new kindergarten after the war in the rubble of Hanover, and it was not until early 1950 that she opened the first purpose-built kindergarten. She eventually began meeting with other kindergarten teachers for a few days each year to deepen their knowledge of the young child out of the anthroposophical view of the human being. This developed into a regular conference which still continues today. It was also the beginning of the International Association of Waldorf Kindergartens, which is now the International Association of Steiner Waldorf Early Childhood Education (IASWECE). Many kindergartens and teacher-training programmes developed out of these beginnings and spread throughout the world. They now include home- and centre-based childcare, parent–child groups and family centres.

Elisabeth Grünelius and Klara Hatterman were researchers 'intuitively feeling their way along out of exact observation of the children in their care. They were visionaries, able to see far beyond their own immediate surroundings, and able to consciously work with the reality of the spiritual nature of the child' (Howard 2006: 3).

Steiner Waldorf education in the UK

Many teachers from other countries heard of the 'new' educational approach being developed in the first Waldorf School in Germany, and they visited to observe. As a result, in 1923, Rudolf Steiner was invited to speak about the Waldorf approach in England, a country which at the time was extremely interested in education. He met with public recognition, not only regarding the education, and was asked to speak about his other ideas on many different subjects. It was at one of these lectures that he met Margaret MacMillan, who, with her sister Rachel (a nurse), had been campaigning to improve the health and education of children. In 1914, the MacMillan sisters opened an 'open-air' nursery school and training centre in Peckham for children from eighteen months to seven years. Margaret had progressive ideas on education and was also interested in an active spiritual life. She attended many of Steiner's lectures and in 1923 invited him to visit her nursery school in Deptford. He described this visit at the time:

> Today I was able to accept her invitation to visit the nursery and school established by her at Deptford, London. Three hundred of the very poorest

population, from the ages of two to twelve, are wonderfully cared for there by her . . . one sees at work in the various classes youngsters who are spiritually active, happy in soul, well-behaved and growing healthy in body. It is an equal pleasure to see these children at play, to see them learning, eating and resting after meals.

(Steiner 1998: 5)

She also gave him her book *Education through Imagination* about which Steiner wrote,

With real genius for education, Miss MacMillan seeks to penetrate the peculiarities of the child-mind. Her book is a treasure chamber of precious observations concerning the child's soul, and is full of guiding hints to those engaged in education. Such a chapter as that on 'The Child as Artisan' cannot be read without a feeling of deep satisfaction'.

(Steiner 1923: 1)

Steiner asked Margaret MacMillan to give the opening lecture and to chair the first of his lecture tours in England in 1923.

Many others attended Steiner's lectures and also heard about the schools being established in Europe. A few nurses and teachers decided to study in Germany or Switzerland with the then small group of kindergarten teachers. They returned to England, joined by others who had already been working in Europe, and became the first established Steiner Waldorf kindergarten teachers in the UK, working in and around the first Waldorf schools which opened as early as 1925.

In the 1960s, Dr Helmut von Kügelgen, who was the head of the Kindergarten Association in Germany, suggested that the kindergarten teachers in England should meet together on a regular basis. They formed a group that organised yearly national conferences to share inspiration and good practice and to meet each other for support. They called themselves the Kindergarten Steering Group, which carried the original impulse to create loving 'gardens' in which little ones can flourish. Later, the name changed to the Steiner Waldorf Early Years Group (SWEYG), which reflected a greater involvement in the wider early-years movement covering all aspects of early-years work including day care, and parent and family work. Early 'years' has now been changed to early 'childhood', which embraces the whole realm of the child from birth to seven and includes both care and education. SWEYG carries and holds the overview for the support and development of Steiner Waldorf early-childhood education and care in the UK and Ireland. There is further current information in Appendix I.

Key points

1. The historical, social and political culture had an influence on the development of Rudolf Steiner's ideas.
2. Rudolf Steiner attributed his insights to clairvoyance and spiritual influences.
3. Steiner wrote about his spiritual, physical and scientific research, which he called 'anthroposophy'.
4. The development of the Waldorf educational approach grew out of a need identified by Emil Molt.
5. Steiner gave thousands of lectures in Europe and England, the transcripts of which became the substance for many books.
6. The development of the child in the light of anthroposophy formed the basis for the educational approach.
7. The self-education of the teacher was as important as the subject taught.
8. Elisabeth Grunelius and Klara Hatterman were the pioneer kindergarten teachers who began what is now the worldwide Steiner Waldorf early-childhood movement.
9. Steiner had a deep influence on the work of Margaret MacMillan.
10. The kindergarten movement spread worldwide, encompassing care and education between birth and seven years.

Reflections

Rudolf Steiner and his work

- What do you think were the political, educational and cultural conditions that dominated in the late nineteenth and early twentieth centuries as Steiner was developing his ideas?
- Can you think of other influences in education which were pioneered at the same time?

The education of the child

- Steiner practitioners see the self-development of the teacher as an essential activity. How relevant does this seem to you?
- Can you identify the qualities that you most appreciated in your teachers when you were a young child at school?

Steiner initiatives worldwide

- The variety and spread of initiatives inspired by the work and ideas of Rudolf Steiner encourage the possibility of a working together of, for example, educators and architects or educators and agriculturalists. Can you see benefits in this?
- Do you know of any other individuals who have initiated such a diverse international movement?

Steiner Waldorf education in the UK

- Are you aware of and have you visited any early-childhood centres or schools based on the work of Rudolf Steiner in your area? If so, what did you find most striking about them?

The beginnings of Steiner Waldorf early-childhood education

- The first Steiner Waldorf school was opened as a response to the chaos that followed the First World War in Germany. Do you know of any other educational initiatives in Britain that were a response to newly perceived social needs at this time?
- What other educational impulses do you know of that are built on a view of child development that extends from birth to age twenty-one?

References

Grünelius, E. (1966) *Early Childhood Education and the Waldorf School Plan*, Englewood, NJ: Waldorf School Monographs.

Howard, S. (2006) 'Extract from an unpublished article, "Rudolf Steiner Asks for Kindergartens", by Elizabeth Grunelius', *Gateways Journal*, 49, p. 6.

MacMillan, M. (1919) *Education through Imagination*, London: Dent.

Steiner, R. (1923) 'Margaret MacMillan and Her Work', *Anthroposophy*, 2 (11): 1–2.

—— (1928) *The Story of My Life*, New York: Anthroposophical Publishing Co.

—— (1965) *The Education of the Child in the Light of Anthroposophy*, London: Rudolf Steiner Press.

—— (1998) *Rudolf Steiner Speaks to the British: Lectures and Addresses in England and Wales*, London: Rudolf Steiner Press.

—— (2001) *The Foundations of Human Experience*, London: Rudolf Steiner Press.

2 Key pedagogical principles

Introduction

This chapter gives an initial introduction to the essential principles (or key concepts) that stand behind Steiner Waldorf early-childhood education. In the chapters that follow you will find descriptions that fill out these principles and show how they are brought into practice. From this summary of what is essentially 'Waldorf' and the subsequent chapters, it will become apparent how these principles have been used to inspire a worldwide educational system, adaptable to many cultures, religions and settings.

Self-education and child development

Rudolf Steiner spoke in detail in many of his lectures about the experiences essential for the healthy development of the young child. He also spoke about the role of the adult, both parent and teacher, and what they should provide to enable this healthy development to take place. Susan Howard quotes Steiner as saying,

> Every education is self-education, and as teachers we can only provide the environment for children's self-education. We have to provide the most favorable conditions where, through our agency, children can educate themselves according to their own destinies. This is the attitude that teachers should have toward children, and such an attitude can be developed only through an ever-growing awareness of this fact.
>
> (Howard 2007: 1)

The role of the educator is therefore seen as shaping and influencing the child's environment, not only through the equipment, activities and rhythms of the day but also through the attitudes of the educators, relationships with each other (children, parents and colleagues) and personal self-development. This means that the gestures, moods, intentions and motivation of the teacher permeate the surroundings in order to create an harmonious, joyful and peaceful environment. If everything that surrounds the child, both visible and invisible, has an impact on the child, then the need to create this harmony becomes essential. The focus on the whole child – physical, emotional, social, cognitive and spiritual, including those gifts and promises which the child brings with them from previous lives, has an impact on how the child is observed and treated, and this reverence for the whole being of the child is what the educator can share with the parents, working in partnership and with love.

Essential principles

In the main, the essential principles as practised in Steiner Waldorf early childhood, where the staff are working with the principles of child development given by Rudolf Steiner, are:

- care for the environment and nourishment of the senses;
- creative, artistic experiences through domestic and artistic activities;
- child-initiated free play;
- the development of healthy will activity;
- protection for the forces of childhood: gratitude, reverence and wonder;
- working with rhythm, repetition and routine;
- imitation;
- the child at the centre.

The list of principles above is neither definitive nor complete but acts as a foundation for the practice. Below you will find some described briefly, and throughout the book you will find references in one way or another to these principles.

Care for the environment and nourishment of the senses

In *The Education of the Child*, Rudolf Steiner said that it is the essential task of the educator to create the proper physical environment around the children.

> 'Physical environment' must be understood in the widest sense imaginable. It includes not just what happens around the child in the material sense, but everything that occurs in his environment, everything that can be perceived by their senses, that can work on the inner powers of the child from the surrounding physical space.
>
> (Steiner 1965: 24)

If educators work with the indications given by Steiner, the sensory experiences that occur, or which are provided in the prepared environment, deeply affect the children's physical and emotional development.

Many times, Steiner referred to the young child as being 'all sense organ'. He said that the young child was like a sack of flour: if you press it a dent remains afterwards. That is to say that what happens in the environment, especially the actions of the people with whom the child comes into contact – shapes the child in quite a literal way. All the senses of the developing child are active. Some, such as the sense of hearing, are active even before birth. Therefore, if the educator is aware that everything the child sees, hears and touches will have a lifelong influence on the child, then the quality of the environment must be carefully considered. For instance, using calming colours on the walls (peaceful pink) and making sure the room is not visually over-stimulating (no displays of work, photographs, posters, letters). That it is not aurally over-stimulating (no excessive noise, electronic gadgetry, tapes, television) and that it appeals to the sense of touch (equipment is made from natural materials such as wood, cotton, silk – not plastic, nylon). Therefore, a clean, orderly, quiet, beautifully and simply decorated room is essential.

This nourishing environment (both inside and out) should also enable the children to have opportunities for their own self-education – such as touch, balance, lively and joyful movement (whether by themselves or in small or in large groups) – and opportunities for constant social interaction. They should have the opportunity to activate their own will through self-motivation, and the environment should be both nurturing and enabling.

The seasons are represented inside, on the nature table, or by simple decoration. Bringing the outside in, and taking the inside out – recycling and cleaning, digging and preparing the garden or vegetable patch, or cutting flowers and arranging vases on the lunch table – are all activities developed and nurtured with the children. They provide a picture of how we can take care of ourselves, each other and the world in which we live, and this picture is nourishing for our senses, our lives and our world.

Rudolf Steiner, in several lectures on education, including Lecture 8, *Study of Man* (1919), described the human being as having twelve senses divided into three groups of four. There are the four foundation senses that tell you about yourself:

1. touch (I have a body with a boundary);
2. life (how well is that body?);
3. movement (my sense of my own willed movements that I can control);
4. balance (am I upright or not?).

The four middle senses tell us about the world:

5. smell;
6. taste;
7. sight;
8. relative warmth.

The four higher, or social, senses tell us about each other:

9. hearing (this tells me about the world in general but in a deeper way than sight, for example);
10. speech (my sense that what I hear from another human being is a language, even if I do not understand that language);
11 concept or idea (the silent space between us that we try to pin down with language);
12. ego (my sense that you are a unique human being too).

Two resources that develop these ideas in more detail are Albert Soesmann's *Our Twelve Senses: How Healthy Senses Refresh the Soul* and Willi Aeppli's *The Care and Development of the Human Senses*.

Creative, artistic experiences through domestic and artistic activities

Artistic and creative activities are those which come from within us: singing, painting, drawing, drama and so on. They are artistic activities which are given wings out of our soul life, our imaginations and our inner creative impulses. Being 'an artist' means to be completely free in the way in which we express ourselves through the various media or instruments, both human or mechanical. The artistic craft activities which are undertaken in the kindergarten are explained in more detail in further chapters.

The domestic arts, or 'life skills' as they are sometimes called, are what are needed to take care of ourselves, each other and the environment. They include personal hygiene and physical care, empathetic care of others in social situations and care of animals and other living creatures. The environment in which we live also needs to be cared for: Where does the dirt come from, and where does it go? Cleaning, mending, cooking and housekeeping, gardening and growing, recycling and protection of the environment – all these are skills which, when learned, last a lifetime. Doing them properly, beautifully, with care and love, help not only to give the young child skills for life but engender a responsibility for the earth and for humankind.

Child-initiated free play

Rudolf Steiner, in a lecture given in 1912, said:

> In the child's play activity, we can only provide the conditions for education. What is gained through play, through everything that cannot be determined by fixed rules, stems fundamentally from the self-activity of the child, the real educational value of play lives in the fact that we ignore our rules and regulations, our educational theory, and allows the child free rein.
>
> (Steiner 1912: 11–12)

In the kindergarten, the children are given opportunity for child-led free play (both inside and outside) (see Fig. 2.1), play arising out of the child's own observation of life, where they have the opportunity to integrate socially and to use their imaginations and fantasy to recreate and work out situations which they have seen or experienced. There is some discussion today on what constitutes entirely free child-initiated play. Piaget described it thus:

> the emotional and intellectual needs of the child are not satisfied if he must constantly adapt to his surroundings. It is therefore indispensable to a child's emotional and intellectual balance that he have an area of activity available in which the motive not be the adaptation to the real but the assimilation of the real to the 'self', without constraints or sanctions: this is play.
>
> (Piaget 1966: 44)

This means that each child's attitude and ability to play is unique, whether they take the lead, follow what others are doing or are immensely creative, wholly imaginative or entirely social. The Steiner setting environment enables this play to take place without adult interference or guidance. The toys are simple, adaptable and made from wood, cloth or other natural materials. They are often collected from nature: pine cones make wonderful trees, shells make plates or credit cards, cloths

Figure 2.1 Play.

draped over frames or tables make houses or boats, a simple circular piece sawn from a log makes a wheel, tray, computer keyboard or piece of toast. These simple toys from natural materials can be anything the child wants them to be: food for the imagination and infinitely adaptable.

There is no unnecessary adult interference in the play, as the adults are involved in their 'work' (often described as 'meaningful activities'), such as preparing the snack/lunch, making or mending the equipment or toys, preparing the room, sewing buttons on a jacket, cleaning the windows, digging the garden or raking the leaves – all the time with an eye on what is occurring around them and able to observe and provide help where necessary. Nor is play 'thought out' beforehand, planned by the teacher or burdened with educational goals.

Steiner educators believe that children find their own learning situations in play; they show more empathy towards each other and develop their social skills. The development of the imagination is an essential aspect of cognitive development and encourages children to become inventive and adaptable and to learn through investigation, exploration and discovery out of their own initiative and inspiration.

The development of healthy will activity

The purpose and direction which adults bring to their lives as free human beings is based in the healthy development of personal will activity. The aspects of the will which need to be developed in the young child cover their instincts, drives or impulses, desires and wishes and motives. This enables them:

- to act for the good (moral judgements)
- to change their thoughts and habits
- to self-regulate and to have control of restraint
- to engage their will in the service of others
- to act as a leader or hold back when necessary
- to be dedicated to a task, persevere with it, and complete it with commitment and determination.

The rhythm and repetition within the kindergarten aids and strengthens this will development in a healthy way, without directly imposing the will of the educators on the child. Providing children with an environment in which they can move in a 'free' way, using their limbs as they are 'driven' to mobility – without instruction or direction – strengthens this capacity. Leaving the children free to 'find out for themselves' and providing them with a role model worthy of imitation in deeds and actions as well as giving stories with a moral or meaningful content, helps them to move from 'doing what they want to do' to 'doing what they need to do' for their own healthy development. At first the children act quite unconsciously in what can be called 'unselfconscious' participation, and only as they become older will they consciously be carrying out actions and activities.

Protection for the forces of childhood: gratitude, reverence and wonder

Enabling the child to have the space and time to weave a tapestry of learning experiences in an unhurried and enabling environment, free from adult instruction, goals and academic restrictions, does mean that the kindergarten years allow the child to follow their own developmental steps and learn at their own pace. Steiner spoke about this in 1923, when he said:

> Although it is highly necessary that each person should be fully awake in later life, the child must be allowed to remain as long as possible in the peaceful, dreamlike condition of pictorial imagination in which his early years of life are passed. For if we allow his organism to grow strong in this non-intellectual way, he will rightly develop in later life the intellectuality needed in the world today.
>
> (Steiner 2004: 119)

In the Steiner approach, the role of the adult is not to instruct but to be a model for the child to imitate. The rhythm and repetition of activities carry the child along, and detailed verbal instruction is not necessary. The stories and songs provide simple imagery which the child can internalise but which do not require intellectual or critical reflection, questioning or explanation by the adult.

Formal learning by instruction and direction is delayed until children are in their seventh year, but before then the foundations are laid through encouraging independent activity and development through the child's self-initiated discovery. It is the educators' task to make it possible for the children to be inwardly creative and outwardly active, and the adults' work is orientated towards development of the children's faculties and skills in the future, not in the present. Therefore, making their progress conscious through photographs, displays or praise is not necessary for the child. Their creativity is 'in the moment' and the outcome is not as important as the process.

Steiner Waldorf early-childhood practitioners work with their image of the child as a spiritual being who comes to earth bearing gifts, and it is the task of the teacher to help each child to unwrap these gifts as they develop. Each human being is seen as being surrounded by love – and the practitioner's gratitude and thankfulness, both for being provided with the opportunity to nurture this being and to the world in which we live should pervade every moment. In a lecture given in 1923, Steiner said that we need to create an atmosphere of gratitude around the children, towards the world and each other, and if we can cultivate this properly within ourselves, then out of this an attitude of thankfulness will develop in the child, and 'a profound and warm sense of devotion will arise' (1988: 128–9).

Working with rhythm, repetition and routine

In Steiner settings, regular patterns of activities create routine, foster a sense of security and self-confidence and help the child to know what to expect. Working with rhythm helps children to live with change, to find their place in the world and to begin to understand the past, present and future. It provides a very real foundation for the understanding of time – what has gone before and what will follow – and helps children to relate to the natural and the human world. Children's memories are strengthened by recurring experiences, and daily, weekly and yearly events in kindergarten (such as festivals and celebrations) are remembered and often eagerly anticipated a second time around.

Repetition helps to support good habits. So, in a Steiner kindergarten, emphasis is given to regular patterns of activities repeated within the day, week and year to provide rhythm and routine. Every day has its own rhythms, which support the day's activities: a 'tidy up' song, for example, might signal the end of one activity and the beginning of another. Seasonal activities celebrate the cycles of the year; autumn might be a time for threshing and grinding corn and spring a time for planting.

If something is repeated often enough, it becomes a habit. These good habits are nurtured, and repetition relieves the necessity for constant questioning and enables a child to learn discipline through repeated good habits, rather than through instruction. Here it is the adult who knows best what clothes the child should wear when going outside in the rain and what food is nourishing and necessary.

Imitation

The anthroposophical understanding of imitation is different from that of some other psychologists (such as Albert Bandura et al.) and their 'learning through observing' model. In *The Child from Birth to 3* it is described as arising from

> the special organic-physical situation of young children: their sense activity, which is intensely receptive to all impressions in the environment, takes hold of the body's physiological processes directly and without conscious processing. Much of what happens in the organs is hidden from observation, but if we look closely we can discover the profound organic impact that sense impressions have and how they manifest in the body as symptoms of stress or relaxation. We can observe the immediacy of sense impression and physical response when we see a mother conversing and playing with her baby during diapering: the baby absorbs the adult's motor activity, facial expressions, and gestures, and imitates them.
>
> (Patzlaff et al. 2011: 19–20)

In Piaget's concept of 'sensorimotor intelligence', what the child perceives goes through their senses into their will activity and is imitated immediately, at the same time as it is observed, with the same objects being used and with the same gestures which the adults are using. There is no intermediary use of mental images.

Lynne Oldfield (2009: 5), described imitation: 'the young child can learn new skills whilst remaining in the dreamlike consciousness, which is natural to his age and is anxiety free. Initiative becomes habit – for imitation is a free deed.' Oldfield goes on to quote research by Meltzoff and Prinz (2002) which establishes that the ability to imitate is present at birth. Further, Oldfield writes:

> We know that imitation occurs on three levels and researchers have noted this in their own way: The child sees and immediately does – synchronic imitation;

The child sees and later does – deferred imitation; The child sees and gradually becomes – this has implications for the soul life. Researchers have concluded that 'perceived action' includes the invisible goals the visible action is striving for, including the mental and emotional states underlying the goals.

(Oldfield 2009: 7)

In other words, if in carrying out an activity in front of children we are carrying negative thoughts or emotions, such as anger or anxiety, young children will pick these up. Similarly, of course, our enthusiasm, confidence and joy in doing will also be picked up. This has profound implications for both the teacher's and children's personal development.

Meaningful adult activity as an example for the child's imitation

In a lecture in 1923, Steiner spoke about the task of the kindergarten teacher, which is to adapt the practical activities of daily life so that they are suitable for the child's imitation through play. He said that the activities of children in kindergarten must be derived directly from life itself rather than being 'thought out' by the intellectualised culture of the educators (see Fig. 2.2). In the kindergarten, 'the most important thing is to give children the opportunity to directly imitate life in a simple wholesome way' (Steiner 1988: 81).

The teacher respects the wisdom of childhood and children's unique mode of experiencing and learning as the first step towards affirming their sense of self. Imitation is one of the most effective and natural means of learning at this age and can be most easily directed when the adults perform their tasks consciously and carefully, repeating the gestures of each action in a rhythmical and natural way. The children imitate the conscious activity of the teacher, in a dreamy and unconscious way. To see an adult at work, perhaps in the activity of carving a spoon, in which care, skill, concentration and perseverance are all demanded, is a wonderful example to the ever-watchful child – a lesson in the sustained application of will power. Children can learn to do quite complex practical tasks, even involving sharp or awkward tools or equipment, if they see them regularly performed with love and care. Teachers therefore carry out their daily tasks in such a way as to be worthy of imitation and remain vigilant that they are providing a model and example at all times. The teacher who sets the example may then have certain expectations of

Figure 2.2 Meaningful adult activity.

the children at different ages. Good objective observation of the children, and knowledge of child development out of anthroposophy, helps them to understand where each individual child is in his or her development.

In a Steiner kindergarten, learning takes place in an unhurried way, through practical activity, play and taking part in 'educational' activities such as:

- movement experiences (ring time, eurythmy);
- handwork (sewing, woodwork);
- housekeeping or the domestic arts (cleaning, food preparation)
- artistic activities such as painting, drawing, crafts, sculpturing, modelling, puppetry, storytelling and so on.

In addition, physical health, equanimity, time and imagination on the part of the adult are needed in order to provide the conditions for the child's healthy development as a foundation for later, more formal, learning. Maths, for instance, is found in baking, setting the table or counting children. Literacy is found in poems, songs, storytelling and puppet plays. Learning takes place out of daily life where the human being and the activities of life are the bridge to the world. Real life rather than virtual experiences help children to connect to the real world; therefore, you will find no electronic gadgetry, media, computers, CDs or television in the kindergarten.

The child at the centre

Putting the child at the centre means not only being in partnership with the parents in accompanying the child on the journey that the child takes from the home to the world via the kindergarten setting but also making sure that, for the child, this journey is a smooth and joyful experience, full of riches and wonder.

It is up to the educator to focus on each individual child at all times, to be aware of each stage of development and each achievement, to help overcome their individual struggles or difficulties, and, as Rudolf Steiner said, to solve the riddle of the child from day to day, from hour to hour and from moment to moment.

Caroline von Heydebrand, who wrote about the child in the light of Steiner's anthroposophy, described the role of educator (parent or teacher) in 'contemplating the child' in *Childhood: A Study of the Growing Child*:

> it should be a spur to the educator ever and again to renew his inner preoccupation with the children in his charge; ever and again to trace the formative powers which shaped this or that particular child. He should repeatedly walk around the child, as it were, contemplating him from all aspects and never weary of deepening a knowledge of his particular laws of growth. One would like to advise all, to whom falls the nurture and education of children, to call to mind at evening before going to sleep the image of the being entrusted to their care. To contemplate him in all minutest details; how he walks, moves and raises his hand, how he laughs or weeps and so on. To sink oneself into this image, not disintegrating it and harassing oneself about it, but contemplatively. . . . Then in time, this child's image in the educator's soul will itself say what it wants to become. The genius of the child, his higher self, will speak; at first softly and then more clearly, telling how he should be cultivated and educated, so that the seeds latent within him can unfold; how the best may be made of what is in him; not the teachers idea of it but the reality.
>
> (von Heydebrand 1998: 48–50)

Not all the principles have been addressed above, but in the following chapters examples of these principles in practice are explained in far more detail. One can see that even though the full Steiner Waldorf early-childhood 'curriculum' contains rituals and practices, specific play materials, songs, stories, festivals, decoration and even the dress of the adults, these are not the essentials. The essentials are found in the principles that underpin the education of the child in the light of anthroposophy. For, as Rudolf Steiner said in many of his lectures, to be an educator, you must:

- observe the children;
- be worthy of imitation in your actions, thoughts and deeds;
- develop your inner life;
- follow your intuitions;
- be fully involved in constant self-education.

Continuous self-education could be through meditating on each individual child every day, preparing the activities and learning the stories, studying child development and creating the environment. This is the work of the educator, and the educator stands (together with the parents) as the bridge to the world.

Key points

1. The role of the educator is to be the shaper of the child's environment.
2. There are twelve essential principles of Steiner Waldorf early-childhood education and care.
3. Child-led, free, spontaneous play is essential for healthy development.
4. A Steiner Waldorf early childhood setting provides a nourishing and enabling environment with adaptable and open-ended equipment engaging the imagination and stimulating self-initiated play.
5. The role of the adult is to be a model worthy of imitation by the child in thought, word and deed.
6. Steiner practitioners work with the image of the child as a spiritual being, bringing gifts for the adult to help them to discover.
7. The educator is to be full of reverence, wonder and joy.
8. Rhythm and repetition are crucial for establishing good habits.
9. Meaningful practical life activities modelled by the adult are offered as an example for the child to accompany.
10. The adult is to be reflective and involved in continuous self-education.

Reflections

The adult as role model

- What self-discovery, self-reflection and self-education would you choose in a position of child educator?
- What self-education would you consider influences the child in your care?

Essential principles

- Which essential principles underpin your practice?

An enabling environment

- What would you consider is a nourishing environment?
- How do sense impressions manifest in your work with children?
- Is your decoration, clothing, equipment, etc., stimulating or calming?

Imitation and example

- How would you consider the role of the adult could influence the child?
- Do you think children should learn through self-initiated discovery?
- How can creativity be encouraged without praise?

Rhythm and repetition

- Which teacher or adult-led activities do you feel should be repeated more than once?
- What good habits could be supported by repetition?

Play as the child's work and engaging the will

- Would you consider your equipment is open-ended and adaptable, enabling imaginative and creative play?
- What would you say constitutes child-initiated play as against teacher-directed play situations?
- What would you consider strengthens and engages the child's will to act?
- What could you provide for children to engage their will activity?

References

Aeppli, W. (1993) *The Care and Development of the Human Senses*, Forest Row: SWSF Publications.

Howard, S. (2007) *Mentoring in Waldorf Early Childhood Education*, Spring Valley, NY: WECAN.

Meltzoff, A. N. and Prinz, W. (2002) *The Imitative Mind*, Cambridge: Cambridge University Press.

Oldfield, L. (2009) 'Imitation and the Cultivation of Empathy', *Kindling*, 16, pp. 5–8.

Patzlaff, R. et al. (2011) *The Child from Birth to Three in Waldorf Education and Child Care*, Spring Valley, NY: WECAN.

Piaget, J. (1966) *La Psychologie de l'enfant*, Paris: Presses Universitaires de France.

Soesmann, A. (1990) *Our Twelve Senses: How Healthy Senses Refresh the Soul*, Stroud: Hawthorn Press.

Steiner, R. (1912) 'Self-Education in the Light of Anthroposophy', typescript, Rudolf Steiner Library, Ghent, New York.

—— (1965) *The Education of the Child*, London: Rudolf Steiner Press.

—— (1988) *The Child's Changing Consciousness*, New York: Anthroposophic Press.

—— (2004) *A Modern Art of Education*, London: Rudolf Steiner Press.

von Heydebrand, C. (1998) *Childhood: A Study of the Growing Child*, London: Rudolf Steiner Press.

3 Child development
The first seven years

Introduction

Rudolf Steiner had much to say about the individual human being, in relation to both his or her physical and spiritual development. The philosophical foundation for Steiner's worldview on many subjects, including the foundations for the development of the human being, is known as 'anthroposophy' (see Chapter 1). In this chapter we will discover how Steiner introduced many new ideas out of his anthroposophical insights. These include the human being as consisting of body, soul and spirit and the various stages of the development of the human being. What follows is an introductory outline of Steiner's complex picture.

A spiritual life

Steiner was convinced about the reality of a spiritual life which included the idea of reincarnation: that the home for each individual is the spiritual world and that one visits earthly existence in order to both learn from and help change the world in which we live. Edmond Schoorel, a Dutch paediatrician, describes it as follows: 'because of the past, we have limitations – our life is predetermined; because of the future, we have the possibility of making decisions about our life in freedom of choice' (2004: 15). Steiner educators see this individuality in each child and are aware that this individuality existed before conception and birth and brings with it, from its past, its own personal destiny. It is the task of Waldorf education to support and enable each individual in his or her path so that they can eventually attain true freedom and purpose in their lives.

The 'threefold' human being

Steiner proposed three constituents which make up the human being as body, soul and spirit. These three divisions are also related to the three regions of the human body:

■ the body: the metabolic limb system (activity following intention);
■ soul: the chest and heart area (the expression of emotion – the feeling realm);
■ spirit: the head (thinking, or the making of mental images).

These divisions work on the whole body in different ways and through the way they interpenetrate, enabling different aspects to develop at different times.

The goal for all human beings is to find the right relationship to themselves and their environment so that these areas of body, soul and spirit find a relationship to the world. The physical body must have the ability to develop healthy organs and a strong immune system. The soul needs to find a positive and secure connection to the world. To enable this to happen, children need to know from their own experience that the world is good, beautiful and true, leading to the wish to help create this in an active meaningful way. The spirit is strengthened through learning to organise and master problems and challenges that occur during life and enables the individual to meet adversity with a positive approach.

Throughout our lives we have to develop and enhance our thinking, our feeling life and our actions if we want to become creative, consequent human beings who realise that the world and everything in it are *our* responsibility. Steiner educators believe that the foundation for this lies in the first seven years when the child is immersed in an environment that enables this to happen through imaginative play, allowing creative experiences of all kinds and the right richness of carefully selected stories. Paramount in this is the adult being grateful for all that is around them, leading to an attitude of thankfulness in the child. At this stage, there is no need for intellectual and academic instruction.

The kindergarten teachers, with respect and reverence, work on creating the right environment so that each child can develop and perfect his or her own healthy physical body (including organs) as well as control of it. Creating the right mood of joy, love and warmth, as well as letting children develop their imagination free from too early intellectual learning, allows the child's life body to form itself healthily in the first seven years. Steiner said that calling too early on intellectual stimulation, as well as on 'awakening' the child through questioning or commenting, would affect this healthy development, and the consequences would show themselves later in life.

The seven-year periods

Steiner not only described in detail the first seven years but also gave a picture of the seven-year periods from birth to death and the different changes which the human being might undergo during these phases. In this book we are specifically concerned with the years of early childhood; therefore, we will only focus on the first seven years.

The first seven years: imitation

Becoming able to stand upright, to speak and to think are remarkable achievements in a period of three or four years, and generally the healthy young child does these without being taught – through instinct and, above all, through imitation. The young child mimics or 'mirrors' every-thing in the environment uncritically – not only the sounds and language of speech and the gestures of others but also the attitudes and values of peers and parents. Freya Jaffke, in *Work and Play in Early Childhood* describes it: 'Every perception is first deeply assimilated, then grasped with the will and reflected back to the outside in echo-like activity' (2002: 10). During the first seven years, it is the role of human beings to perfect the development of their physical body in their own time and aided by healthy external influences and the right environment.

The second seven years: imagination and creativity

Following Rudolf Steiner's beliefs, towards the end of the child's first seven years, various changes take place, the most prominent being the formation of the second set of teeth, which indicates that the physical structure is complete and that the child has worked on fully inhabiting his or her body and being. This shows itself too with the development of a new and vivid imaginative life and a readiness for more formal learning , which is provided through an artistic approach, achieved by an imaginative and creative classroom experience.

Phases within the first seven-year period

Birth to three

The faculties and abilities that unfold during this period are those of walking, speaking and thinking in words. Children learn these skills through imitation of other human beings. The sense of 'me' is particularly strong before three, and it is with the development of 'me' in relationship to 'the other' that difficulties arise, often known as the 'terrible twos'. Saying 'no', temper tantrums and hitting often emerge at around the same time as children begin to develop their sense of self, when they become more aware of their own will but need to learn to control it and the effect that it has on their surroundings. Their will needs to come into harmony with their environment.

The child learns to say 'I' for the first time, and the image of themselves as separate to others takes some time to work through. In play, children tend to socialise 'alongside' the other, out of imitation. They need others to show them what to do and observe unconsciously in a dreamy state before recapitulating it out of imitation, in play. (This is why the adult as role model is so important.) 'Naming' is an important part of speech development, and coming to terms in an active way with what is being named impresses an understanding of that 'named' item or activity in a real way.

In Steiner settings, play with babies is intimate: they play with light, sound and, from the start, with the humans around them – exploring through touch from the moment of patting the breast when feeding to playing with their own feet and hands. 'Peek-a-Boo' is a favourite, and they attach to objects such as a doll or cloth. Their play is not yet social, and although they love to play 'house', they need mother to 'do it too'. Their play with objects such as blocks has no purpose other than to build towers (knocking them down and building them up again) or to place logs in a line. It is not thought through and needs no outcome: the joy is in the moment.

During this time, the physical development of the child undergoes its biggest change. The large-headed baby, reliant on others for its survival, becomes upright, the torso begins to fill out and the legs grow strong, leaving the arms free to carry out the activity that follows the intention.

Three to five

Following Steiner's ideas, educators believe that the formative forces which were busy working in the head region now move to the breathing area (heart and lungs) of the 'middle' realm: the chest. This is why working with the gentle, calm 'breathing' rhythm of the hour, day, week, etc., is so important. Memory and imagination begin to flower, and this is the period in which children can really use all their imaginative forces in socialisation and in spontaneous play, born out of the moment and generally prompted by an activity or object they encounter.

Play, during this period, is more imaginative and physical – full of exploration of themselves in the world. The children have the capacity to transform what they have at their disposal, anything from their surroundings, into whatever they need them to be (see Fig. 3.1). Using their imagination they see a piece of wood as a tray or a shell as a credit card. Their play also undergoes transformation, moving from one subject to another in a somewhat chaotic fashion – the train they are travelling in could become a restaurant, transforming again into a boat.

Symbolic and representational play increase, and the children need others to participate – play becomes social, and roles are allocated: 'you are the mummy and I will be the baby and you will look after me!'

Figure 3.1 Imaginative and physical play.

Children begin to express their feelings: 'Poor baby, I will get you some milk'. They need equipment to support their play when imitating domestic activities such as food preparation and people at work, recreating events and using the physical body and language to express their intention, desires and needs. They need to have the space to run, jump and balance, climb and master their physical needs and capacities. They also need to feel their boundaries, both physically and emotionally.

Physically, the growth of the body centres on the middle realm: the torso lengthens and fills out before the legs and arms become strong as children gain control of their bodily functions.

Five to seven

This is the last developmental step before the 'school years' or when more formal education begins. It is the time of great change and transformation of the child in many areas. The healthy child hopefully gains mastery and control over his or her body. At this stage, the formative forces are working with the metabolism and the limbs, and gaining mastery over movement is of vital importance. This includes both small and large motor skills, skipping, climbing and taking risks, being able to do up zips and buttons, cut with sharp knives, use needles to sew and use woodwork tools.

Children's inner life also undergoes a major change at this stage, when their imagination seems to leave them, and they need to immerse themselves in real-life activities for a while until this transformation takes place. What changes is the ability to be able to bring their own inner picture, the experiences and understanding which they have gathered, to their play. Their intention needs to be fulfilled properly. Instead of using the forces of imagination to transform any stick into a fishing rod, they say, 'I need a fishing rod, so I need a stick *this* long and some string to use to catch fish'. Then they capably spend ages making the fishing rod so that it 'works properly' often needing or sometimes asking for the help or guidance of the adult to refine this. They take initiative and plan their play, discussing endlessly what will happen and how in fine detail before carrying it out. For example, I found that the older children in my kindergarten were the ones who planned the puppet show, gave others roles, would perform and play the music, sell the tickets, etc., spending ages in the preparation, and then the planned show would last no more than a few minutes. They do not need prompting from outside, or an event they have seen, but they now can develop play ideas based on a memory of a previous experience.

The children's imagination is rich and full: imaginary worlds are created alone or with others, and their play is social, including the beginnings of mastering authority, for instance when playing the zookeeper in charge of the animals. Empathy play begins too, when 'being the other' takes place. They plan their games, put rules in place and 'direct' the play as if from outside. Their inner life is active, and the ability to imagine and create their own stories internally – sometimes to be expressed in play or in drawing – or even to tell the stories themselves is exciting to watch. Language is fascinating to them, and playing with rhymes, riddles and using story language to describe events is wonderful to experience, particularly at a group time such as over lunch. Children, especially boys, delight in tying things together at this stage, and joining pieces of wool to 'wire up the house' shows the linking of concepts in the developing motor skills.

In a Steiner setting, the developing will now needs to be directed at tasks that help others, ourselves and the environment. Participation in watering the plants and preparing the earth for planting, or in cooking the meal is expected and helps also to develop a sense of respect for the earth. Concentration on a task, following things through and listening to authority all help towards good citizenship and social responsibility at a later stage.

Physically, the child's limbs lengthen and become strong, the body also lengthens and the 'puppy fat' tends to disappear. The head is more in proportion to the limbs and the child grows confident in his or her intention and direction, socially and physically.

Foundations for a healthy life

Steiner Waldorf education, if seen from the anthroposophical understanding of the human being, can create a healthy foundation for the whole life. Understanding this is the responsible educator's tool. Therefore, as Steiner says, one must not educate in order to imprint 'learning' on the child but leave them as free as possible to learn and develop as individuals. It is only through this freedom that human beings can realise the impulses that they brought with them from before birth.

Key points from Steiner's anthroposophical insights

1. Steiner said that the human being consists of body, soul and spirit (the threefold human being).
2. Each individual has a past and a future, both from and to a spiritual life.
3. The goal of the human being is to develop the thinking, feeling and active (doing) life equally.
4. The seven-year periods address different capacities and developmental milestones in the individual.
5. Speaking, standing upright and walking and thinking are developed through imitation of others in the first seven years.
6. The development of the imagination can be aided by providing open-ended toys, space for free play and told stories.
7. The first seven years include three separate developmental phases.
8. Formative forces work on different aspects of the physical, emotional and intellectual being.
9. The development of the will can be aided by providing meaningful tasks, activities that enhance the well-being of ourselves, each other and the environment.
10. Imitation is inherent in every child and present on three levels: synchronic, deferred and 'becoming'.

Reflections

The development of the human being

- How would you acknowledge and address the development of the different areas of body, soul and spirit?
- Would you say that your physical, emotional and intellectual capacities are addressed equally?

Spiritual life

- Have you considered the possibility of having a spiritual life?
- How would this manifest in your view of the child as having a spiritual past and not simply being the physical presence which you can see.

Seven-year periods

- Each of the seven-year periods addresses different aspects of the human being. What are the most important aspects in the first seven years?
- What needs to be provided in the environment to aid the physical development of the child?
- How can we be a role model for the child to imitate? What do we need to develop and work on in ourselves?

Development of the will and the imagination

- Which daily activities and tasks could be done in the setting with which the children could join in?
- What equipment could be used by the children for open-ended play both inside and out?
- Which activities enhance the well-being of ourselves, each other and the environment?
- What can we provide which can aid children to use their fantasy and imagination?

References

Jaffke, F. (2002) *Work and Play in Early Childhood*, Edinburgh: Floris Books.

Schoorel, E. (2004) *The First Seven Years*, Fair Oaks, Calif.: Rudolf Steiner College Press.

Steiner, R. (2008) *Educating Children Today*, London: Rudolf Steiner Press.

4 The environment

Introduction

In this chapter, we describe the various environments that may make up the Steiner Waldorf early-childhood setting. The sensory experience of the child has a great significance for his or her development. For this reason, the Steiner kindergarten environment requires much careful thought and detailed attention and is distinctively different from most settings for young children. We shall consider the effect on the young child of beauty, colour, natural materials, seasonal and other decorations, the equipment for domestic activity indoors and the complimentary environments outdoors. The materials available for the children's play in the Steiner setting are described and the adults' role as an important part of the environment will be discussed.

The first sight of a Steiner kindergarten room can make a striking impression on an adult visitor. The soft colours and textures, the natural materials, the use of flowers, branches, seed pods and other seasonal decorations and the homely sight of simple kitchen equipment, mending baskets, even a spinning wheel, all combine to show that this is a special place. Steiner kindergartens are situated in many different kinds of buildings including purpose-built spaces, church and other community halls, adapted houses and temporary structures such as yurts. Wherever it is, for the Steiner practitioner, one of the first priorities is to make it both a beautiful and a functional place. These are spaces for children designed to be visually attractive, to be practical, to be nurturing and to exemplify a core principle of the Steiner Waldorf early-childhood curriculum – enabling children to be involved in the everyday tasks of living. It is a space that will give the visitor much information about what the children actually do in a Steiner Waldorf kindergarten.

Why should the environment of the young child be beautiful?

As discussed in Chapter 2 the Steiner practitioner sees young children as a work in progress in all areas. Their physical bodies, for example, not only have to grow larger, their inner organs also have to reach their completed forms, and much of this development takes place in the first seven years of life. Rudolf Steiner suggested that young children are such sensitive beings that everything in the environment will have an impact on them, most directly on their physical development. 'It is the right physical environment alone which works upon the child in such a way that the physical organs shape themselves in the right way' (Steiner 2008: 30).

If this is the case, then a beautiful environment will support harmonious and healthy physical development. Even for an adult to be surrounded by gentle toning colours will have a positive and soothing effect on mood, whereas strident clashing colours and busy patterns might encourage feelings of nervousness, anxiety or even aggression.

As Oldfield (2002: 100) writes, 'Clearly the sight of the kindergarten room makes an impact on the new parents. This impact makes an even deeper impression upon a young child.' The decoration and arrangement of the Steiner kindergarten are designed to work on the senses of the young child so that he or she feels calm and safe. A spectrum of colours can be imagined which has soft pinks, violets and peach colours at one end and browns, sludge greens and maroons at the other. It stretches from the heavenly to the earthly colours. In the Steiner kindergarten it is the heavenly colours that predominate in the decoration of the room, with a rosy pink as the main colour theme. Busy patterns are avoided so that the eyes can rest and the child feel soothed. Even in the rented church hall where everything has to be packed away every day, time will be taken to hang up curtains in that special shade of pink and to arrange things beautifully.

Natural materials

In a Steiner setting, there will be an emphasis on natural materials: wooden furniture, fabrics of cotton, wool and silk and, where possible, natural floor coverings. This natural, simple theme will be reinforced in the choice of play equipment for the children: wooden planks, play stands and crates, with plain cloths and knitted woollen ropes for build-ing dens. Wicker baskets full of items from nature such as pine cones, conkers, stones, shells and logs will be there to furnish games with food, money and any other small parts that may be needed. Very simply made dolls, puppets and dressing-up clothes are available to bring games and stories to life. Appendix I includes a list of typical equipment.

Why is there such an emphasis on natural materials? The answer is summed up by Jaffke (2002: 19): 'Natural materials greatly extend the range of experience of the child and enhance his or her sensitivity. Even the simplest objects provide the child with food for the imagination.' The solid wood table and the pure silk fabric cost more that the petrochemical-based substitutes, which reflects the instinctive feeling that the natural and authentic are more valuable. Why is this particularly important for small children? Steiner pedagogy sees them as particularly vulnerable and sensitive to their environment, although they do not have the con-sciousness to express it in ways that adults can easily understand.

Authenticity is a key word. Young children are at the beginning of learning about the world, and their constant endeavour is to make sense of their experiences – to build a coherent picture. Therefore, authentic, true experiences support them in their task and encounters that are not 'real' do not give coherent sensory experiences. For example, something may look like a wooden table, but if it is actually made of plastic, when you pick it up it is not heavy enough, the texture is too smooth and, significantly, it does not reflect the warmth of your hand in the way that wood does. Warmth in the young child's world is vital both physically and emotionally, and the Steiner practitioner sees natural materials providing warmth in a way that man-made substitutes do not.

It is worth taking into account warmth as part of the children's experi-ence of their environment. Feeling warm but not too hot is related to feeling relaxed, mobile and flexible, so the practitioner would like the rooms to feel cosy, especially when the weather is wintry outside. Nevertheless, taking the children outside for some of every session, whatever the weather, is part of the Steiner ethos, and parents will be encouraged to ensure that the children are dressed warmly and with effective wet-weather gear when necessary. This is all part of providing an environment for the children that helps them to feel comfortable.

Smell, taste and hearing

Apart from the smell of good food cooking, most commonly soups, wholegrains and bread with highlights of honey-sweet birthday cake and spicy festival biscuits, the environment offers a spectrum of authentic natural smells for the child to experience. The smells that seem most distinctive to me as a practitioner are those of hot beeswax, both when the candles are dipped and when they are lit, sheep's wool being washed (this is often needed for toy-making), and lavender being prepared for making lavender bags for use in the kindergarten and as gifts to take home.

The sense of taste is fed by organic food, prepared in simple ways and based on a variety of whole grains with fresh fruit and vegetables and herb teas. The encouraging social dynamic of the kindergarten snack time, when the whole group sits down together to share a meal, helps many a child to find a lifelong liking for foods that she has not met or come to enjoy before. Again, the emphasis is on giving the child a high-quality sensory experience.

The acoustics of indoor spaces for children are given careful consideration as high ceilings with hard surfaces can make children's voices echoingly piercing. Steiner settings often use soft furnishings and untreated or rough-sawn wood to help soften the sound of busy children at work and play. Our ears are constantly receiving information, much of which we come to screen out. This screening process, as with all the sense organs, is something that children are not able to do innately. By taking care of their sensory experiences, as the Steiner setting tries to, young children can be given a healthy start and a strong foundation from which to cope with the complexities of modern life when they grow older.

The Steiner Waldorf setting will often sound quite noisy with the busy sound of children playing, the harmonious sound of singing and reciting together, the social sound of the group eating a meal together, but there will be no sounds of electronic toys or music. There will be times when the voice of the adult predominates, singing and telling stories, but this will not be the case when the children are engaged in their self-initiated play. There will be plenty of music, provided by voices but also by simple, often homemade musical instruments and by a small stringed instrument called a lyre (very much like a small hand-held harp), which will be tuned to the notes of the pentatonic scale. The lyre has a very pure tone, and the notes of the pentatonic scale all sound tuneful together, 'in tune' with the emphasis on harmonious sense impressions. Finally, but vitally, there will be moments of silence that arise naturally when a candle is lit for snack time or story, perhaps at the end of the 'ring time' of songs, games and poems, and at the end of a loved story well told.

A place to live and work

A Steiner Waldorf early-childhood setting should not only be an environment that is beautiful and relaxing but also a functional place where children can safely be part of the everyday work that is needed to take care of, equally well, the people and the spaces that they inhabit. This need for practicality is reflected in the environment. Kindergarten rooms usually include a kitchen with all that is needed for preparing and clearing away meals and for washing dishes and laundry. Where there are no facilities in the room, ingenuity is used to bring all aspects possible of the 'kitchen work' into the children's main space. Vegetables will be chopped, bread made and dishes and dolls' clothes washed. The cups, plates and kitchen paraphernalia will be arranged on shelves which the children can reach so that they can be involved in all these activities from getting things out through to putting them away again – seeing domestic tasks through to completion.

How comforting it is for the children when they arrive in the morning to see that the things needed for preparing the snack are being got out. They know that there will be food when they are hungry and that they are welcome to participate in its preparation. What lessons are subconsciously learnt when they see and help with the housework that keeps their room fresh and clean, from washing, oiling and wax-polishing the wooden toys and equipment to watering the plants and scouring the copper kettle with squeezed lemon halves dipped in salt? They may see adults making and mending toys, and many kindergartens include a woodwork bench where children can work on their own simple projects under the practitioner's supervision.

Bringing the seasons indoors

Most noticeable in the kindergarten room is the seasonal or festival table, sometimes called the nature table (see Fig. 4.1). This is often in a corner

Figure 4.1 The harvest table.

and arranged so that the children can sit around it for story time. This table, cared for by the practitioner with the help of the children, will reflect what is happening at that particular time of year. Plain coloured cloths will be spread and draped to give horizontal and vertical spaces on which seasonal material, such as leaves, flowers, moss and twigs will be arranged. There may be figures such as a young girl clad in green to symbolise spring or a man with a long white beard and cloak of sparkly material as frosty old King Winter. You might see other appropriate animals, birds or insects and artefacts for different times of year: lambs of white sheep's wool in spring, coloured paper birds or bees made of alder cones, wool and tissue in summer, lanterns in autumn and so on. These will often be made by the children, and in addition to the ones that decorate the room, they will take home their handiwork to decorate their own homes. In some cases, the nature table includes some sort of representation of the four elements: earth (maybe a crystal or some moss), air (a mobile of snowflakes or butterflies), fire (a candle or lantern) and water (a dish of water or a 'pond' or 'river' made from a piece of blue silk).

Vases and pots will be placed on the snack table, filled appropriately for the time of year, perhaps with bare branches or evergreens in winter, budding twigs in spring, flowers in summer and coloured leaves and seed pods in autumn. Again, colour may be used that seems right for the time of year, for example in a mat or cloth on which the vase stands. The practitioner might work through the colours of the rainbow from shades of green in spring through yellow to red for midsummer, autumnal shades of purple, maroon and brown to a deep blue for midwinter. Many variations are possible, but all this work with colour and decoration forms a familiar pattern that the child will recognise from one year to the next.

Displaying children's work

Painting and drawing are valued activities in the kindergarten, but you are unlikely to see children's art work displayed around the room. One reason for this is that the Steiner practitioner wants the emphasis to be on the children's activity rather than the result. However, the practitioner may use his or her own artwork to decorate the room or choose a suitable seasonal subject from sources such as calendars. These will generally be paintings in soft and gentle shades, including, perhaps, illustrations from the traditional fairy tales that are told or the yearly round of festivals that are celebrated.

One particular painting holds a special place in many Steiner Waldorf kindergartens and early-childhood rooms throughout the world, and this is *The Sistine Madonna* by Raphael (1483–1520). This shows a representation of the Virgin Mary carrying the Christ child towards the viewer. Behind her is a cloudy sky which a closer look reveals to be full of children's faces. She steps between a pair of parted curtains, and she carries the child so that he is facing us. They both look directly out of the picture without hesitation or fear. One experienced Steiner early-childhood practitioner writes:

> To me, the picture of Raphael's *Sistine Madonna* is a picture of the ultimate educator. The way in which the Madonna holds the child, how she is present with the whole of her body. Her eyes look out into the world, observing without judgement. With her body she covers the child, but with an open gesture. The child faces the world. She carries the child in her arms, but she does not restrain the child. If it needs comfort and security she is there, but she does not demand to get her own needs satisfied. The child rests in her arms, completely relaxed but

alert, observing the world without emotional opinions. The child doesn't need the mother's confirmation because she is there, at peace, and yet in constant motion.

(Heckman 2008: 41)

Whether or not to display this particular picture will be a personal decision by each practitioner. One can see this painting as a symbol of the child moving from the heavenly reams into earthly existence, in the care and protection of an archetypal figure representing the adult. Many practitioners feel that the presence in the room of this particular picture is a support and protection both for them and for the children in their care. Others find that it carries too strong a connection to the European Christian tradition and that the Caucasian skin tone and features of the figures do not fit in our settings that represent a diversity of cultures and ethnicities. Some add to or replace it with other more multicultural images representing a young child held in the mother's, father's or grandparent's protective gesture, free to follow his or her own destiny into the world.

Completing the child's environment

There is more to children's environments that just the room in which they play, eat and join in with indoor activities, and some description is due of other spaces that make up a Steiner Waldorf setting. These may include transition spaces such as entrance lobbies, cloakrooms, washrooms and toilets. Here you will find the same attention to detail, to beauty and to function that is reflected in the main room. The entrance is what the children see first every day when they come to kindergarten or school, so it must be welcoming, with a warm gentle colour scheme, natural materials and soft textures and some seasonal decoration.

Next come the areas where outdoor clothing is kept. As there is a real emphasis on the children being dressed well for going outdoors there is plenty of practical storage for clothing and footwear. Everything from snowsuits to sunhats will need to be accommodated so that the children can access their belongings and keep them tidy in a practical way. Getting dressed to go outside is a major activity in its own right, particularly in winter, and requires proper facilities and space. The Steiner practitioner considers that it can then be a source of real learning for the children, through mastering fine and gross motor skills and developing social skills, and it fosters patience and perseverance.

In toilets, handwashing facilities and nappy-changing areas, the same care and attention will also be taken to make them lovely places which are well looked after. They are places that every child will visit every day, and the impressions that such areas make on children are often very long-lasting. Many people have memories, sometime not very pleasant ones, of the toilets of their first school and the impact that these made on various senses!

Steiner pedagogy suggests that self-care – one might say respect for one's own body – can be built up by the mood in which these activities are arranged and supervised by the practitioner. As with cloakroom time, the emphasis is on taking time to do things properly, for example, maintaining a good handwashing routine. The Steiner Waldorf practitioner believes that by encouraging a responsible and careful attitude towards one's own body at this age, a more respectful attitude is likely to the self and to others in later life.

Outdoor environments

The garden

Outdoors, as with the indoor spaces, beauty and practicality must both be served, and the practitioner is responsible, sometimes with the help of parents, for looking after the garden. Most settings will have an outdoor space of some kind, and there are impressive examples of how many important things can be packed even into a small space. There will be paths and surfaced areas for playing and working. In addition to grass, bark chips are often used as ground cover. These are a pleasant, natural material which children enjoy playing on and with. They need regular raking and replenishment; along with sweeping the paths, this provides a frequent task for the adults when they are outside with the children, especially at the times of year when there is less work to do in the garden beds.

Most settings try to grow things that the children can see gathered and used in the daily life of the group, even if it is only a pot of herbs that can be snipped for making tea or adding to soup. Where there is the space, there may be large flower and vegetable gardens and even perhaps some small-scale grain-growing so that the children can be part of the real harvest experience of making their daily bread. Some settings and schools have animals, such as chickens, and some are even on farms where the children can see and be involved in the daily life and care of livestock. There will also most likely be a bird table, a compost heap and a washing line – all necessary to everyday life. Many tasks – cleaning and washing, food preparation, mending and making of all kinds – can be done outside and, as natural imitators, the children will absorb the attitude of the practitioner to the outdoor environment in a very thorough way that will require little in the way of direct instruction in environmental education.

Where there is the space, you may find swings and slides, but you may notice that, when possible, climbing frames will be made using logs, trunks and even trees that are growing there – natural materials again (see Fig. 4.2). A tangle of branches is much more of a climbing challenge than a regular climbing frame. There will also be 'loose parts' (Nicholson 1971: 30–4) which the children can use to create their own structures in the garden – logs, planks, twigs and stones – in addition to the traditional sand pit and an area where children can dig in the earth and use water to create that most creative and attractive of substances, mud.

Figure 4.2 Outdoor play.

Beyond the garden

The wider environment can be explored regularly by the whole group, especially when there is only a very small secure garden for the children to play in or even no garden at all. When a kindergarten class is part of a bigger Steiner school, then walking around the school grounds to see the outdoor activities of the older pupils in the school can be a regular and endlessly fascinating activity. There is also the option of travelling further into the local area. Rural groups may have familiar country walks and favourite playing places in woods, meadows and streams. In the town or city, there are parks to be visited or even walks to the shops to buy things that are needed. In order for such expeditions to be carried out safely, the practitioner will be sure that there are sufficient adults and will teach the children, again by imitation and example, how to walk in a 'crocodile', cross roads and respond to adult signals. These are all valuable lessons to learn alongside an interest and enthusiasm for what the local area has to offer. On these expeditions there will be an emphasis on rhythm and repetition so the routes and routines will soon be familiar to all the children.

The enabling environment

All the parts that make up the environment of the Steiner Waldorf early-childhood setting are designed and used to support the core principles of the education. In every way, the children are encouraged to feel safe and comfortable, to enjoy time and space for self-initiated play and to take part in everyday life. The environment enables the children to develop their innate capacities out of their own interests and at a rate that is individually appropriate. It supports healthy interest in the world, including a healthy social sense and a healthy aesthetic sense, and, through the practical activities that engage the children, it builds their confidence in being able to make sense of and manage their world. In the next chapter, we shall go on to explore in much more detail how the adults, as part of that enabling environment, support the learning and development of the children.

Key points

1. The Steiner Waldorf early-childhood environment has some distinctive characteristics that spring from the emphasis on the child's sensory experience.
2. The Steiner setting aims to combine beauty and practicality as the children will be involved in the everyday tasks of living.
3. Key elements include a rosy pink hue on the walls and an emphasis on natural materials in order to give authentic coherent sensory experiences.
4. Parents will be encouraged to dress their children well enough to enjoy the outdoors every day, whatever the weather.
5. How the environment smells, tastes and sounds is important.
6. The environment will be arranged so that the children can help with kitchen tasks such as food preparation and laundry.
7. There will be a seasonal table using colour and symbols as well as natural materials to 'bring the outside indoors'.
8. The room may contain art work by adults, including paintings representing the adult and child, such as Raphael's *The Sistine Madonna*, but the art work of the children will not be displayed.
9. Areas other than the main room of the setting show the same attention to beauty and practicality.
10. Where possible, the garden of the setting will include space for all kinds of outdoor work as well as for play with natural and unformed materials such as branches, sand and water, and the practitioner will regularly take the children beyond the garden.

Reflections

- Why should the environment of the young child be beautiful?
- What is distinctive about the environment of your setting?
- Is it beautiful, giving a cared-for and harmonious impression?
- What colour scheme do you think is ideal for an early-childhood setting?

Natural materials

- Is it important to you that children use and play with natural materials?
- Can you think of situations where natural materials are not practical?

Smell, taste and hearing

- How do you see children in your setting responding to smells, tastes and sounds?

Bringing the seasons indoors

- What is there in your room that 'brings the outdoors in'?

A place to live and work

- Would you describe your setting as functional?
- Is it designed to draw the children into such things as domestic work?

Displaying children's work

- What do you have displayed as decorations and art work, and why?
- What is your response to the Steiner practitioner's attitude to displaying children's work?

Completing the child's environment

- Is there coherence and beauty in the decoration of all the rooms that the children in your setting use?

Outdoor environments

- What do you consider the essentials of an outdoor space for young children?
- Can you think of ways in which your outdoor environment could give children more of an experience of nature and of the human being working with nature?

Beyond the garden

■ What would you need to put in place in order to take children on outings from your setting?

References

Heckman, H. (2008) *Childhood's Garden*, Spring Valley, NY: WECAN.

Jaffke, F. (2002) *Toymaking with Children*, Edinburgh: Floris Books.

Nicholson, S. (1971) 'How NOT to Cheat Children: The Theory of Loose Parts', *Landscape Architecture*, October, pp. 30–4.

Oldfield, L. (2002) *Free to Learn*, Stroud: Hawthorn Press.

Steiner, R. (2008) *Educating Children Today*, London: Rudolf Steiner Press.

5 Imitation and example

Introduction

In this chapter we shall focus on how the young child learns best and how this capacity is nurtured in the Steiner Waldorf early-childhood setting. We shall be calling on the picture of child development already laid out in Chapter 3 and illustrating how the child's natural, innate ability to imitate is used as the primary learning method in the Steiner setting. Emphasis is laid on the child's environment as a source of learning and on the attitudes and behaviour of the adults in it. An explanation is also included of the child's changing relationship to imitation within the first seven years.

Finally in this chapter we shall look at the importance of the self-education of the practitioner, the challenges and opportunities that this brings and the tools that may be useful in developing the art of educating the young child.

The natural imitator

The newborn child is at the beginning of a complex developmental journey. On the way there are many skills to master and capacities to learn, all of which each child will do in his or her own way and time. For this potential within children to be gradually released, the most important requirement is human company. It is through their experience of other people that they learn to stand upright and to walk, and also to speak, and only after children have learned to speak can they begin to think clearly in words and so develop from being an unconscious being

Figure 5.1 Imitation in ring time.

into being a conscious one. This is to say that it is through their experience of human beings and their wish to imitate them that children become free human beings themselves and able appreciate the humanness of others.

The wonderful ability to imitate is born with children and is the foundation stone of their efforts to make sense of the world during the early years of life. It comes from their openness to everything around them and from their innate desire to respond to the world with movement. In deep unconsciousness, they absorb everything that is around them and actively mirror it back through their own individuality. That is why the environment that surrounds young children is so vitally important. Their openness and unconsciousness mean that they need to be protected not least because what they are absorbing and reflecting back are forming their physical body, in particular their neurophysiology, in ways that will affect them throughout their lives.

As Steiner pedagogy sees it, all adults have a great responsibility when in the presence of children and have the opportunity to contribute to their healthy development. In response to children's unconscious commitment to imitate their surroundings, adults must be fully conscious of all actions in the presence of children because, from the young child's position, the adult will always and inevitably be modelling how human beings behave.

Not only is each child's imitative response to the world unique as it is funnelled through his or her individual personality, it also fits in with a pattern of child development that applies to every child. Children imitate in different ways at different times, and knowledge of this is another help to us as we endeavour to support and nurture them. As they become more awake, so their ability to imitate changes, and this gives different learning possibilities of which the practitioner needs to be aware.

As Goddard Blythe (2008: 179) writes:

Babies are born mimics . . . [They] will imitate adult gestures like sticking out the tongue only a short time after birth . . . humans are born with the . . . capacity to assimilate movements, feelings, and gestures through simple imitation, and . . . this early language becomes part of the vocabulary of a mirror neuron system, which is able to sense and recognise the needs and feelings of others – the origins of sympathy.

Children respond through movement

As children gain control of their movements so they imitate the movements of the people that they see: blinking and yawning, for example, followed by waving and clutching, followed in their own good time by rolling, crawling, pulling themselves upright and staggering in forward motion. Parents experience much joy in playing games which rely on imitative capacities with their babies. Mothers instinctively speak to their babies in a language that Goddard Blythe (2008) calls 'motherese', and which, with its short repeated sing-song phrases is designed to be copied. Nursery rhymes follow on, equally full of rhythm and repetition, accompanied by gestures and giving great delight to young children (see Chapter 7).

Adults have the consciousness to make judgements and can decide not to take an interest in something. Adults can decide that something is not worthy of attention. They also gain the ability to unconsciously shut out distractions in order to focus on what seems to us to be essential for understanding and managing the environment. Steiner practitioners believe that little children do not have this ability. If there is noise and chaos around them, they are not able to shut it out, and their capacity to understand and make sense of their world is undermined. Their attention and energy are spent on dealing with, and trying to make coherent, much that is quite unworthy of their attention. This is how Oldfield (2002: 101–2) explains it:

> She is, as it were, united with sensation and therefore deeply affected by what it conveys, and her psychological development is influenced by the immediate surroundings. Carl Jung emphasised that the less conscious we are, the greater the impact of experience upon the psyche, and the more potent is that initial impact in determining future behaviour.

It is as though young children are worshippers and their god is the whole of their surroundings. They enter into it with such reverence that it becomes part of them, and, because their interest in and response to their environment is expressed through movement, they imitate. They are so at one with the world that what they see, they do and become.

The Steiner practitioner holds that the first responsibility of an educator is to protect children and fill their world with activity worthy of their worship and imitation. Such a world will start small (usually centred on the mother) and slowly grow, ideally along with the child's pace of development, as declared by Winnicott (1987) in his chapter entitled 'The World in Small Doses'. Young children are very interested in developing their movement skills and are, indeed, almost constantly moving. They love to be active, and we can see more and more purposefulness in this love of action as the child grows older.

In the Steiner setting, it is felt that too many words from the adult can soon overwhelm the child, for actions truly speak louder than words in any situation concerning young children, and a barrage of words will have little effect except to confuse the young child. This is an important foundation of creative discipline. Aged less than five years old, children have a general willingness to follow the active adult leader. This is summed up by Patzlaff and Sassmannshausen (2007: 82):

> Regardless of his own faculty for autonomous development, the young child needs role models in all areas for imitation and orientation. The inner attitude and outer behaviour of grownups form the first and most elementary learning environment whose imprint is left on the child's later biography. Parents and educators can fulfil this task of being role models through self-development and conscious reflection on their actions.

Working with imitation in the early-childhood setting

In the Steiner Waldorf early-childhood setting or kindergarten, all the adults will use imitation and modelling in preference to direct instruction in order to work with the child's natural way of learning. They will also take full advantage of the young child's natural wish to be active.

For example, when the children come into the kindergarten room in the morning, the adults are already busy preparing a soup for the kindergarten meal. There are vegetables to scrub, peel and chop and herbs to snip. Everything will be arranged so that the children can work with the adults. Either there will be something to stand on so that the children can reach into the sink to scrub the carrots with the small brushes provided or bowls of water will be put on the low tables where the children can easily reach to help. Chopping boards, bowls for compost scraps and for chopped vegetables, knives, peelers and scissors will be set out alongside the vegetables and the herbs. If there are two adults, one may be scrubbing and the other busy with peeling and chopping. Some children love to be involved in the splashy task with the scrubbing brushes; others prefer to use a peeler and a knife.

The children are drawn to join the active scene that they see on their arrival. With just a gesture, the practitioner can indicate to the enthusiastic children that the aprons are waiting on their usual pegs to be put on, and there is also a place ready for handwashing. A child who overlooks these essential preliminaries or skimps on them by not tying up the apron or not washing and drying the hands well is gently guided back and helped to do these things properly. A gesture and a familiar phrase such as 'Good cooks put on their aprons and wash their hands' is usually enough, but if it is needed an adult will accompany children to the handwashing sink and wash hands with them: wetting, soaping, rinsing and drying together.

The actual tasks of scrubbing, peeling and chopping are carefully modelled by the adults. The object is not to do the task as quickly and efficiently as possible but to do it with full attention and in a way that the children can take up. As this task occurs every week, the children will have plenty of opportunities to grow into the skills involved. The adults are close at hand all the time and can reach out to help as necessary so that the use of sharp tools such as peelers, knives and scissors is well supervised. Experience shows that children from the age of three rarely cut themselves if they are given proper tools of the right size for their hands and if the mood is one of careful engagement.

This does not mean that this is a solemn and silent affair. There is conversation, perhaps familiar songs, and plenty of smiles. Some children naturally come with news from home to share, and this is listened to by the adults and responded to with a warm and encouraging nod or a short comment. In the Steiner setting it is not likely that the practitioner will question the child to extend the topic. There is time and space for the child to say what he or she has to say but this is not looked upon as an opportunity for guided learning. We are making soup, and that activity is the focus. Strangely shaped vegetables may be commented upon. The bowl for the compost scraps will be pushed towards the child who has produced a pile of carrot peelings. There is no need to discuss the fact that these peelings will go on the compost heap and that the compost will go to nourish the garden. The children will be there when the compost is put on the heap and when the rotted compost is emptied onto the garden beds. They will be engaged in the natural cycles of growth, decay and regrowth that are involved, and they will absorb knowledge of them subconsciously. Later in their education, after the age of seven when they have left kindergarten, they will learn consciously about the science and methods behind what they experienced when they made soup and grew vegetables in kindergarten and understand it more thoroughly because they already know it through their previous activity.

It may be that not every child does come to help with the soup-making, or some may stay for a very short time. However, the centred activity and the mood which it engenders will also influence the free-play space into which all the children will gradually drift as the tasks of food preparation finish. For example, at the beginning of one bright summer morning, a teenage helper was sent outside with a tarpaulin, some rope, hooks, etc., and asked to put up a sunshade under which the children could play later when we went outside. He became completely absorbed in the challenges of the task he had been given. He climbed up and down, measured, pondered and screwed in hooks, tried things out and pondered again. Some of the children watched out of the window for a while, but in a short time, all began to play. They played with a great intensity, designing, discussing, building and rebuilding with an unusual seriousness. Later, during the outside playtime, this mood lived on with quite different self-initiated outdoor games. This was imitation, not of the young man's activity but of his attitude to his task.

The same kind of imitation takes place in the home when the parent or carer is busy with work that a child can make sense of – something where it is obvious that what the adult is doing makes a difference to the perceptible world. Doing a batch of ironing, cutting a hedge or painting one's nails falls into this category but reading a book, even for study rather than pleasure, does not. If the adult work takes place where the child can also play, then there may be a 'can I help?' phase, followed by a session of busy play nearby. This gesture of the adult engaging in looking after the world while the child helps or plays alongside is one of the mainstays of life in the Steiner early-childhood setting as explained by Jaffke (2000: 29–30):

> All normally developing children receive their guidance and their impulses for their actions, their play and behaviour from the adult world. In going about their work, teachers are aware of each individual child in their care. The children are left quite free to imitate. All of them may emulate the adult in their own time and in their own way as they complete their learning stages. If the adult activity around them is sufficiently broad and if it is repeated often enough, all children will find what they are unconsciously seeking for the stages of their development, in relation to their own imitative capacity.

The adult as a model

We have already mentioned how children, up to the age of five or so, imitate unconsciously, without in any way thinking to themselves, 'I will follow the adult.' In contrast, the Steiner practitioner is required to be very conscious, to be calm, active, organised and attentive. Those responsible for preparing the vegetables for the soup have been careful to ensure that all the equipment is either there for the children to join them in their work or is easily available to the children. Constantly leaving one's work to fetch forgotten items or to deal with other things is considered to be distracting for the children and disturbs the focus. So does an adult who is rushing to get the work done and out of the way as soon as possible or who is cutting carrots clumsily or absent-mindedly while really thinking about something else.

Often the practitioner will begin an activity when the children are already present. For example, after the soup is put on to cook and equipment has been washed up, there is time to make some progress with the lanterns that are being constructed as it is November and the children can see that the darker time of the year is coming. First the practitioner makes sure that there is a cleared table space ready for the work. Then all the things that might be needed for the work have to be gathered: scissors, paper, tissue paper and glue. Some children naturally become engaged in this preparatory part of the activity. Once the work on the lanterns has started, other children come along and ask to work on their own lantern, which they must fetch from the shelf. They might also need to find themselves a chair if lots of chairs have gone 'off to play'. At some point, it will be time to tidy up so that snack time will come at its proper time. So the adults begin to tidy away their own work and to put away the tools, handing some to the children who will know where they are stored. Even if the children do not stay to tidy away the craft activity, beyond putting their own lantern back on the shelf, it is important that the adult sees it through to the end, putting things away neatly rather than stuffing everything into the cupboard in a jumble.

What have the children learned through imitation?

In this typical kindergarten morning, the children have, out of imitation, engaged in fine and gross motor skills while they have helped to prepare the food that they will eat and the lanterns that they will light and carry. They have been with an adult who has modelled respect for, and the proper use and care of, tools and who has shown what creative miracles our hands can perform. Hopefully the adult has been an example of joy and enthusiasm for the tasks in hand, even those that have to be repeated every week, or every day. There may also have been an opportunity for the children to see someone who attempts something without succeeding at the first attempt – while cutting out an intricate pattern in a lantern, things may go wrong and there may have to be a repair or a search for a different way to do something from the original plan. To strive, to fail, to find a way forward and to complete the task are all attributes that children learn by imitation and example.

Different ways of imitating

It is already evident that there are different kinds of imitation going on in these examples. There is the direct imitation that takes the place of instruction in the Steiner early-childhood setting, when the adult does something and the child immediately does likewise. This is especially visible during ring time, which occurs regularly in the daily rhythm. It is a time when the whole group comes together, usually after a session of activities and play, and the children are led by the practitioner in a flowing sequence of songs, poems and games, full of movement as well as speech and song. Here the adults 'do' and the children join in, and everything is learned through imitation. There is no need to 'teach' any part of it, the children will just pick it up through the repetition.

In order for this is happen, the material has to be well chosen and well put together, and there has to be sufficient repetition and time for the children to become absorbed. In a surprisingly short time, they know what they are doing. Usually the children will learn a new ring time more quickly than the adults – it comes naturally to them. As they follow the lead of the practitioner they are unselfconsciously participating in the actions and gestures they see. They do it because they are natural imitators, because ring time happens every day at the same time and is part of their life of habits, and because it is designed to be a happy fulfilling activity for children to be engaged in. An example of a seasonal ring time suitable for a group of three- to six-year-olds is included in Appendix III.

Indirect imitation is happening when some children are playing busily while the adults and other children are engaged in some task. They are all carried by the mood created by the engaged atmosphere, as the whole group was when the young man was struggling to build the sunshade. It is most important that the adults in the setting are aware of this. Tensions and dissatisfactions felt by the adults soon influence the children and in particular undermine their ability to play freely. This means that the Steiner practitioner has to practise setting aside their own troubles and preoccupations when they are with the children and really focus on the work in hand. The social activity of the group is especially dependent on the kind of mood created by the adults, and this is why it is the children's self-initiated play that is immediately affected.

Delayed imitation

Delayed imitation is often seen when the children are at play. For example, on the way to kindergarten they have seen cement being mixed for a building project, and a cement mixer is constructed as part of the play. One of the older classes in the school has developed a passion for volleyball and are to be seen every day playing in the main school playground, and suddenly there is a 'volley ball net' rigged up out of a blanket draped over ropes tied between two trees in the kindergarten garden and jump-ing children with their hands in the air.

This is where the repercussions of screen viewing can also appear. Sometimes a scene from a DVD that has been viewed just by one child in the group can have a big impact on everyone as the child tries to make sense of something that has unsettled him or her. For example, we have seen a morning dominated by play and talk about 'aliens', which was very unsatisfactory because the concept was unclear to the children, even those that had seen the DVD, and no one really knew what to do, only that the key ingredients were fear and aggression. When this sort of thing appears, the practitioner has to be ready to step in as a very sensitive play facilitator. Many of the challenges that manifest in the setting will come as a result of the children's capacities as unconscious mimics of everything in their environment, the positive and the negative. This emphasises the necessity of an observant awareness in the adults and a readiness to respond to emerging situations with positive possibilities for imitation that will overlay the negative. The need to work with parents on a shared view of child development is also vital.

The transition to the next step

The younger the child, the more immediate an imitator he or she will be. If one child in a group of one- and two-year-olds begins to cry, it is very contagious. The moment that a child tries to offer comfort instead of crying with the unhappy one, perhaps by bringing a toy or by attracting the attention of an adult to the needs of the situation, a new phase has been reached. Nevertheless, the transition from being an imitator to being able to resist following the lead of another is a very gradual one. While it is a wonderful thing to be able to work with the little child's innate imitative capacities, there is also a need to support children towards the next phase of being able to resist the need to unconsciously copy. This is prepared for in the kindergarten in a playful way by intro-ducing games that include moments of anticipation – clapping games, for example – when everyone knows what will happen next but is encouraged, through the game, to refrain from doing it until the moment of holding back has been absorbed.

In the Steiner kindergarten with an age range of three- to rising seven-year-olds, the children gradually become more aware as they grow older. The three-year-olds joining the kindergarten are in the middle of the highly imitative phase, and most of the time the good habits of the older children in the group will be all that is needed to teach them what they need to know to fit into the rhythms and routines of the class. Around the age of five, however, the children discover that they can choose not to imitate. If a three-year-old accidentally falls off a chair at snack time, several others will do likewise. But the older children in the group will know that snack time is a time for sitting still at the table, and they should be able to stop themselves falling off their chairs. It happens in ring time too when the older children suddenly decide that they can change the words to a song. Here the experienced practitioner makes sure that there is a place for these new possibilities within the context of a game, but that the need for ring time to proceed smoothly is acknowledged by these more awake older children: 'We all need to help the younger children.'

One way to characterise this progression is to see it as the step from the three-year-old naturally *wanting* to do as the adult does to the six-year-old *knowing* that he *should* do as the adult does. The age of imitation is moving towards to age of authority. Adults need to work sensitively with this transition. The new capacities of the older children must be found a useful place in kindergarten life, and this is where the mixed-age group of three- to rising seven-year-old children gives many opportunities for the oldest children to experience that they are making a really valuable contribution to the life of the group. A very clear description of the development of imitative behaviour over the first seven years can be found in Jaffke (2000: 13–19), and the task of working with the older children in the group in particular will be returned to in subsequent chapters.

Older children can be seen not only helping the younger ones by behaving well – joining in familiar ring-time material and not falling off their chairs at snack time – but also by helping in more active ways. They may be able to do up zips and buttons and to tie shoelaces and apron strings for those not yet able to. They should be able to set the table for the shared meal – counting children, chairs and place settings – and to do other tasks unaided that they have repeated many times with the adults. They may go on errands to other classes, sometimes with notes written by the practitioner and sometimes with messages to remember. There will even be those special and long-remembered moments when they remind the adults of something that has been forgotten! How wonderful it is if children can make this kind of positive contribution to their environment. When they can see what a difference their help has made, they need little verbal praise as they feel their own reward. In fact, too fulsome expressions of gratitude by the adults can distract them from this genuine feeling. Often a smile is thanks enough. And what a good example has been set for the younger children in the class to follow when they reach the exalted age of six.

An experienced Steiner practitioner knows that in these mixed-age settings it is vital to engage the oldest children and to maintain their good will by giving them challenges that will stretch them and rewards that will satisfy them. The attention of the adult to a conversation initiated by the child is often the best reward, for example, as the older children wash up with the adult while the younger ones are playing. As they move from the age of imitation towards the age of authority, they crave this serious adult attention and acknowledgement that a new stage is approaching. It is dangerous to the health of the whole group to neglect the needs of the older children or to find only negativity in the new skills that they are not yet quite in control of. Not least because the younger children in the group will, of course, imitate them.

The self-education of the adult

In Steiner practice, much is asked of the adult once the primacy of working with imitation and example is accepted. If everything that the adult does, says and even thinks in the child's company is an example which will be taken in and modelled back in some way, a great moral responsibility is implied. It is the adult's duty to provide a protected environment in which it is safe for children to find sources for imitation and where warmth of interest in them will encourage their natural activity. Remembering that children are doers rather than thinkers, the practitioner has to overcome the normal adult tendency to intellectualise life and provide activity rather than words for the children to imitate.

Every adult brings individual strengths and weaknesses to the early-childhood setting. One may really struggle to enjoy certain kinds of tasks in, for example, housework or gardening. Another may feel quite inadequate when it comes to singing with the children. Children have strengths and weaknesses too, of course, and here are opportunities for adults to provide examples of taking on tasks that seem distasteful or difficult, and doing them with good heart. Our lives are sometimes full of things that we must do but don't really want to, and this will also be the case for young children in their future lives. Steiner practitioners believe that if they can be an example to children of adults who try to love what they have to do and to overcome their weaknesses and inclinations, then the children have a better chance of being able to do this themselves when they are adults.

Young children become what they experience, and what we are, as educators, is more important than what we say. To strengthen and educate adults to take up this great responsibility, Steiner settings and trainings focus on developing the powers of observing the children and match this with a deepening interest in the study of child development. This is important continuous professional development to which all educators need to give time and attention.

They also encourage practitioners to develop their own artistic abilities, believing that knowing what the individual child and the group needs and responding in the moment are artistic skills as much a painting a picture or writing a poem. Steiner pedagogy acknowledges that education is an art, and time is set aside for art and craft activities in the life of the practitioner outside the classroom. A well-crafted kindergarten morning is as great a piece of art as a sculpture and requires just as much creativity.

The spiritual background to Steiner Waldorf education also plays an important part in the self-development of the adult. A spiritual background to education is certainly not unique to Steiner education, as Oldfield (2002: xxii) says: 'Froebel, Montessori and Steiner . . . held the spirituality of the child in the highest regard, and for Rudolf Steiner in particular this was always meant to be the starting point for the teacher's relationship to the children in his care.'

As discussed in Chapter 3, Steiner saw the human being as composed of a physical body, a soul life of feeling and a spirit which we become most aware of through our 'free' thoughts, that is, through thoughts not attached to our sense perceptions. We know that we can control our thoughts to some extent, and Steiner encouraged the cultivation of this faculty as a uniquely human strength. He also found it self-evident that something of the inner spiritual nature of everything is revealed in its physical appearance and that, through practise and training, this can become more easily read by the observer. The Steiner practitioner has an inner path of training to follow and uses this in preparing for work with the children. As Nicol explains (2010):

> The kindergarten teacher also prepares inwardly for the group. Usually a picture is formed of each individual child and taken into sleep, or a verse said for a particular situation or child in need. Often this results in improved behaviour or

a story or activity which could help a particular situation comes to mind – and very often, as in a child study, a particularly difficult issue is resolved – a miracle.

Key points

1. Young children's devotion to their environment is so great that they absorb it and then respond by imitating it.
2. It is the responsibility of the Steiner practitioner, therefore, to create an environment that is worthy of this devotion and imitation.
3. The activity of the adult provides the role model for the child, rather than words alone, and in the Steiner setting children learn through imitation rather than direct instruction.
4. The work of the adults is undertaken with care and attention so that the children may either imitate the activity directly or the mood behind it.
5. In this way, the quality of the children's self-initiated play benefits from the adults' attitude to work.
6. The children watch and may help the adults see tasks through from the first preparations to the final tidying away. They may also see the adult make mistakes and put them right.
7. Ring time is a daily example of children learning through imitation.
8. The younger children in the mixed-age kindergarten will see the older children as role models so it is very important that these older children are helped to be good role models.
9. By the age of five a child is developing the ability not to immediately imitate others. This holding back is a skill that will be essential for the next stage of education.
10. Steiner pedagogy sees education as an art; therefore, the practitioner or teacher is an artist always using creativity.

Reflections

Learning through imitation

- How have you seen young children learning successfully through imitation rather than direct instruction?
- Are there things that you do in your practice that you would not want the children to imitate?

Being a role model

■ Do the adults in your setting undertake tasks with care and attention? Is this more of a priority than speed and efficiency?
■ How do you see the adults in your setting creating a mood which supports the engagement of the children in play or in teacher-led activities?

Working with a mixed-age group

■ Do you see younger children imitating older ones?
■ Do you see this as a positive or negative experience?
■ How would you encourage older children in a group to be a good example to younger ones?

The child imitates what he has experienced

■ What examples have you seen of children imitating in your setting, things that they have seen elsewhere?
■ What has been positive and what negative in this?

Education as an art

■ Do you see education as a creative art on a par with painting or writing?
■ Can you imagine that artistic work would improve your practice?

References

Goddard Blythe, S. (2008) *What Babies and Children Really Need*, Stroud: Hawthorn Press.
Jaffke, F. (2000) *Play and Work in Early Childhood*, Edinburgh: Floris Books.
Nicol, J. (2010) *Bringing the Steiner Waldorf Approach to Your Early Years Practice*, London: Routledge.
Oldfield, L. (2002) *Free to Learn*, Stroud: Hawthorn Press.
Patzlaff, R. and Sassmannshausen, W. (eds.) (2007) *Developmental Signatures: Core Values and Practices in Waldorf Education for Children 3–9*. New York: AWSNA.
Winnicott, D. W. (1987) *The Child, the Family and the Outside World*, London: Pelican.

6 Play at the heart of the Steiner Waldorf setting

Introduction

There is much talk of 'the play-based curriculum', and there are indeed parts of the rhythm of the Steiner kindergarten morning that would come into the category of 'playful learning' or 'guided play' (ring time, for example). However, this chapter discusses why self-initiated free play is such a vital part of a child's development and looks at the harm that might be caused by the lack of it. We look at what is needed to stimulate and nourish essential deep play and at the place of the adult in this child-led activity. Examples are given of how the behaviour of the adults in the setting affects the children's play and how adults can become successful play facilitators while still leaving the initiative with the children.

What is self-initiated play?

All Steiner Waldorf settings give time and space, both indoors and out of doors, for children's own self-initiated free play. As Oldfield (2002: 96) writes, 'In the Waldorf kindergarten, every effort will be made to provide conditions in which play can flourish – sufficient time, appropriate space and equipment, but most of all an attitude of respect towards this most magical characteristic of childhood' (see Fig 6.1).

'Free play time' has traditionally been invested with much importance in the Steiner Waldorf kindergarten. This is the time when the children can express themselves without any adult guidance or goals. The adults' part in this activity is, at least on the surface, a minimal interaction. It is not the practitioner's task to, for example, set up a shop with goods to

Figure 6.1 Self-initiated play.

buy and tokens to buy them with and to invite the children to join in. Nor is it likely that an adult will move into a game initiated by the children in order to guide or extend it in order to give more 'learning opportunities'. Oldfield (2002: 90) writes:

> Children at play need to have their privacy respected. Prompting questions and intrusive comments also have a tendency to pull the child out of the condition necessary for this quality of play. (Imagine yourself writing a book, composing a tune, painting a picture – and being constantly interrupted with questions and comments – 'What is it going to be?'; 'Aren't you clever!'; 'Make it a bit bigger . . .').

Steiner practitioners believe that this is the place for real freedom (within the bounds of safety and sociability) and real choice for the child. It is interesting to observe that, until the age of around five or so, the choice of what to play and how to play it is unconscious. A young child may, for example, set off across the room and trip over a stick lying on the floor. This prompts him to pick it up and to begin to play with it. Maybe it becomes a walking stick and the child becomes a traveller needing shelter, food and clothes to sustain him on his journey. He comes upon travelling companions and so there is a game happening. On the other hand, another child, or the same child on another day, trips over the same stick, picks it up, ties a string to the end of it and is a fisherman attracting others to search for sticks and strings and do likewise.

In both cases there has been an interaction between the individual and the environment that has led into play. The play is self-initiated, but not a conscious choice of the children engaged in it. You might say that it just happened, or that it spontaneously emerged from the response of the child to his surroundings.

Choice

Choice does not feature much in other areas of the kindergarten, and conscious choice is generally avoided. The practitioner will not say, 'What would you like to play with today?' or 'Who would you like to play with?' At snack time, there is rarely a verbalised choice of food, for example, though there may be a plate arranged with pieces of different types of fruit that is passed around the table. The Steiner practitioner's view is that choice is an unnecessary burden for the young child and what the child really wants is for the adult to know what is best for him, not to be given the responsibility of making decisions for himself. Steiner practitioners believe that children who are not weighed down by inappropriate choices when they are young will be more capable and secure in making sensible decisions when they are older. The practitioner knows the children and observes them closely. He or she will know their tendencies and interests and will plan the environment and the activities out of that knowledge.

Free-flow play

If play is the place for real freedom in the young child's life, and that freedom, before the child is five, at least, is manifest in an unconscious passage through the play environment, what are the characteristics of this self-initiated play? This will be a free-flowing experience with one game often transforming seamlessly into another. The fishermen from the last example may go on to cook their fish over a fire or build a boat which then becomes a house or even a spaceship to facilitate visits to other planets. Alternatively, the children may become the fish themselves and go swimming off under that table where the snack is being prepared and then turn into cooks helping in the kitchen. One game metamorphoses into another, the equipment in use changes its purpose (a den that collapses may become a bonfire, or a fishing rod may become a space telescope), and the players themselves may move from one group to another, perhaps taking parts of their play with them to tack onto another game. One does not hear young children engaged in this kind of play say, 'That game is finished. Let's start another one.'

Another characteristic of this kind of play is the children's identification with their play, their devotion and attention. Through their unconscious engagement in their activity, the game is as real to them as anything is, and the ability sufficiently to detach themselves to know that it is only a game and they are not really going to reach Jupiter usually comes after the child has reached the age of five. The ability to lose oneself in a game remains long after this but there is a level at which children know that they are 'only playing'. For example, a group of children are playing together on the other side of the room. They are gathered around one child who is the only one seated, and they are holding a large log over her head. The adult can only see that this is a log, but the children can all see, hear and even smell a hairdryer, because they are at the hairdressers.

Before moving on to look at why this kind of play is so important, consider the ending of a playing session. The experienced practitioner will have skilful ways of bringing play to a close that does not burst the 'play bubble' of the younger children in the kindergarten. What is noteworthy is how satisfied the children are at the end of a session of this deep play in which they have been so fully engaged – as satisfied as the sculptor stepping back from the final touch given to a piece of work or the poet finishing the last line of a poem. Although there may be nothing tangible to show for their labours, for the children will certainly have been working hard, they will have that same feeling of artistic satisfaction. What they have just done has flowed out of the deepest core of their unique being, from their spirit, one might say. As Rudolf Steiner (1996: 80) says:

> The difference between a child's play and an adult's work is that an adult's contribution to society is governed by a sense of purpose and has to fit in to outer demands, whereas the child wants to be active simply out of an inborn and natural impulse. Play activity streams outwards from within. Adult work takes the opposite direction.

Why is this kind of play so important?

Steiner practitioners advocate that what children unconsciously choose to play and how they choose to play meets their needs. In a social situation, within a few essential social ground rules, it is trusted that the play that emerges is the play that the children require for their development, and it happens at the right time for them. Play provides the individualised curriculum, the bespoke tailor-made learning experience that every child needs.

Clouder and Nicol have the following to say about the value of play for the young child:

> Play is a learning activity through which we first experience cooperation, risk and creativity and begin to discover the physical laws and structure of the world. Play helps our cognitive and kinetic development, and enhances our problem-solving abilities, aesthetic sensitivity and linguistic skills. It teaches us to manage our frustrations and joys, and strengthens our sense of purpose and determination. It encourages self-motivation, helps us find our individual personality and facilities empathy for other [see Fig. 6.2].
>
> (Clouder and Nicol 2008: 6)

Figure 6.2 Creative play.

'Outside in' and 'inside out' play

Some play is clearly being used as a way of processing experiences. One might call this play from the outside working inwards. Another kind of play just as clearly reflects new capacities that children find in themselves. This would be play from the inside working outwards. It can also be seen how the two are intermingled and how both kinds are children's attempt to find meaning and coherence in their world.

'Outside in' play bubbles up out of the power of imitation discussed in the previous chapter. It might be that hairdressers or fishermen, or even space exploration in conversations, books and films will provide play themes as well as real-life experiences. It can provide a way for children to digest traumatic experiences. For example, we have heard that young Palestinian children play games about suicide bombers and martyrs. As Winnicott (1987: 144) writes, 'Whereas is it easy to see that children play for pleasure, it is much more difficult for people to see that children play to master anxiety, or to master ideas and impulses that lead to anxiety if they are not in control.'

Even children with happy settled lives bring macabre themes into their play from time to time: 'I died and you buried me'! Play is the safe place to explore such things. It is also the safe place for the 'good' child to experience what it is like to be naughty, and many children also have times when they love to play being a baby or a toddler, often as a recapitulation just before a new phase in their development.

Steiner practitioners see 'inside out' play is often a good way to observe phases of development in children. Five- and six-year-olds can so often be seen tying equipment and themselves up in a network of knotted ropes. This is just the age when children begin to connect concepts – if I do this, then that will happen – and what is all this tying and knotting if not an outer representation of this new inner capacity. At the other end of the early-childhood age range, at birth and for the first year of life, the head is the most complete part of the child's physical body, and this is when the round soft ball is a favourite. Of course, games involving balls remain popular with children of all ages (and some adults), but the baby loves to hold and feel the ball and experience its roundness. Toddlers are happy building and demolishing with their bricks, reflecting their inner work of breaking down and rebuilding cells as they do a remarkable amount of growing. This is all part of the individually tailored learning process that begins in babyhood.

If the flow of play in a group can be allowed to run as it will, the sense of purpose and perseverance of the children will be strengthened. It takes effort and initiative to play out the games that arise, and having the time and space to do this will build the ability to take on tasks and see them through in a creative way in later life. Steiner explains it as follows: 'The urge to play, the particular way in which a child plays, disappears and sinks below the surface of life. Then it resurfaces, but as something different, as the skill to adapt to life' (quoted in Jaffke 2004: 26).

What does the Steiner practitioner see as the consequences for children who are not allowed enough time for this kind of self-initiated play? They will struggle to digest their experiences and make sense of their world. They will lose opportunities to strengthen their imagination and creativity and to practise their developing faculties at crucial moments. Problems will arise later because the social situations that are thrown up by group play will not have been explored. Most importantly, children's self-worth will not have been acknowledged as they have not been able to make their unique contribution to the world. As Jenkinson writes (2001: 18),

> Success in sociodramatic play, skill in the use of good interventions, good interactions, and flexibility all develop social competence and prepare the child not only for integration into but for life itself. Good players learn to take their cue from others; are prepared sometimes to lead and sometimes follow, and, crucially, are willing to learn: *to change, to adapt and to move on.*

What supports self-initiated play?

Chapter 4 discusses the physical environment of the Steiner setting which is designed to enhance the possibilities of proper play. The two most vital things that play needs are time and space. Children need time within a healthy rhythm (see Chapter 7) for their own self-initiated play, and they also need the space that gives them freedom to move and create what they need.

Nicol (2010: 29) explains the importance of time and space for play in the kindergarten:

> The time for play . . . is given a large part of the kindergarten morning. The 'empty' space into which the children come (inside or out) leaves huge scope for

the child's creativity and imagination. There is enormous freedom for their play – nothing is previously set up, no hospitals, post offices or hairdressers, no intentions for the children's learning, no teacher planning or preparation – just an empty space provided, an atmosphere of industry and calm and simple toys, natural materials and playthings provided should the children need them.

In the Steiner kindergarten, where the children stay until they are rising seven years of age, there is no written literacy and numeracy work or formal education of any kind. This begins when the children move on into the main school at the age of six, if there is a Steiner main school for them to join. There are important teacher-led elements in the Steiner kindergarten, ring time and story time, for example, but there will always be two substantial playtimes during the course of the session, one indoors and one outdoors. No formal learning needs will be allowed to encroach on this sacred time.

The Steiner Waldorf setting has long emphasised the importance of outdoor play in nature as a nurturing, inspiring and educational experience for all young children, and this is given time every day.

'Loose parts' play

Having the right kind of playthings is also crucial to the kind of deep play experiences that Steiner settings promote. The theory of 'loose parts' described by the architect Simon Nicholson states that 'in any environment, both the degree of inventiveness and creativity and the possibility of discovery are directly linked to the number and kind of variables in it' (quoted in Tovey 2007: 74). The equipment of the kindergarten, indoors and outside, will be full of things that can be used in many different ways, such as planks, crates and blankets for building play spaces and very simple dolls, puppets and representations of animals that can be used for small world play. You will not find intricate building sets that have to be put together in a set way or dolls that have fixed expressions, for example. All this equipment needs to be kept in good order and stored where the children can fetch it for themselves. One might think of the kindergarten as a beautiful and well-ordered storeroom for builders', engineers' and artists' equipment. Part of the joy and the learning experience of creative play, especially for the older children, is the satisfaction of finding, gathering and putting together all the 'loose parts' that the game requires. In fact, it quite often happens that this part of the game takes up all the time – the spaceship may be built but the journey not embarked upon, the small world may be set up but the puppet play never played. The game has been worthwhile in its making.

Alongside time and space as essentials for play there is the openness of the adults to seeing new ideas unfold from the fertile ground of the children's playtime. New ways of using the familiar things appear every year in the kindergartens, as, for example, a game leads to a set of shelves being laid on its back and used as a removal van. A mango from the fruit bowl becomes the troll for 'The Three Billy Goats Gruff', and the cloak-room becomes a house of many rooms as cloths are strung across from one coat peg to another. The practitioners quietly appreciate the deep fount of originality that lives in children playing freely. They rejoice that this originality will, if allowed to flourish now, still be available to these children when they are adults facing the unique problems of the future, beyond our imaginations.

The adult as a play facilitator

As discussed, the adult has a serious responsibility for creating and maintaining the mood in the Steiner Waldorf early-childhood setting. The best accompaniment to support deep play in the children is the calm adult, actively and joyfully involved in meaningful work. For much of playtime, this is all the 'facilitation' that the children require, especially if the adult is able to trust that the children's play has a real value to them and will give them what they need. The practitioner needs to be interested in the children's play but not too much head-down in the work. He or she needs to be aware yet able to hold back and see how situations develop. As Jenkinson writes, 'Play can be a powerful diagnostic tool as well as a therapeutic agent. We adults need to notice our children's play, be brave enough not to deny or forbid it, and try to respect the child's need for it' (2001: 14).

For example, what might seem to be an argument or a fight brewing can sometimes be resolved by the children themselves if they are given the chance. It is so much more worthwhile if this happens giving children the opportunity to develop their own social skills and not to always be reliant on adults to sort out their difficulties. The Steiner practitioner often finds that ears are the best helpers in judging the state of the play. Hearing is a sense that has a special capacity for discerning the truth of situations, and a sensitivity for the timbre of voices, as well as for volume and pitch, is a great asset. The adult can hear when stress begins to creep in, as opposed to excitement, and then it is necessary to make the fine judgement as to exactly when it is necessary to intervene. How long can the resolution of the problem be left in the hands of the players?

Knowledge of the individual children is a great help here, built up out of past observations of their behaviour when playing and in other situations. It is fundamentally important for the practitioner to work on deepening this understanding through observing the self-initiated play of the children. Another great support to good play, and to the adults' feeling of trust in the natural process of the play, is a culture of good social habits amongst the children.

Golden rules

Steiner practitioners find that a few 'golden rules' consistently applied are important. These will be framed as positively as possible and make sense to the children. For example, 'Here we are kind to each other' is a good starting point which no one can argue with. The emphasis is always on the positive. Young children are doers and need to hear first what they may do, not what they may not. The basic rule, 'Here we are kind to each other' leads to many opportunities to show the children, through a story or a reminiscence at the meal table, for example, as well as through one's own actions, what constitutes kindness.

Golden rules can also be very practical. The old-fashioned wooden clothes airer is a much-prized piece of equipment for house-building purposes. In a setting there will never be enough of these, so the sensible 'golden rule' might be that only two clothes horses can be used in each 'game', that is, each group of children playing together. This makes perfect sense to the children because they can see that there are not enough for everyone to have six to build with, although they might wish that they could. It is also a rule that, once established by the adults, the children will be able to administer themselves as they understand the justice of it. They will also soon discover the advantages of combining with a neighbours' game in order to double what is available for their constructions. Golden rules can also reflect a care for the environment. 'Tables that go off to play must be covered with a cloth.' This avoids unnecessary scratching of wooden tabletops and will be combined with regular oiling or waxing and polishing of the tables as part of the routine of cleaning and care in the setting. 'We take care of our dolls' encourages care of each other, as dolls are representations of people. Some practitioners call the dolls in the settings 'doll children' or 'doll people' to make this clearer and spend time dressing and arranging them to be part of a festival or to join the audience of a puppet play.

The Steiner practitioner knows that it is important to make the golden rules simple and few and then to keep to them, showing that they are respected. It is very undermining for the child and for the discipline of the whole class if the appropriate and sensible rules are not kept. However, it must be said that children have a natural and unconscious knowledge that not everyone has the same needs and capacities and will accept changes in the rules that fit with their instinctive knowledge of their fellows. For example, younger children, new to the group, who do not understand social niceties, will receive different consequences if they hurt someone in play to six-year-olds who have been in the group for two years and know both how to behave and how to restrain themselves. Children who meet and play together every day are very good at teaching each other the golden rules.

Intervening in play

Not surprisingly, there are times when more active intervention in play is necessary. Socially inappropriate and aggressive behaviour are not allowed to go unnoticed and unchecked, and the experienced practitioner decides when help is necessary. The health and security of the whole group must be given priority even if there are children who are very new and inexperienced in social play or who are, perhaps, digesting some trauma in their family life. As young children are such strong imitators, they should not be given a poor model. For example, children who are repeatedly hurting others must be helped towards better behaviour and the whole group must see that such behaviour is not acceptable.

Creative discipline: immediate responses

Depending on the age of the child, various creative approaches to discipline are applicable. For the youngest children, distraction to another activity is the first resource. Children love to be active, and being active with the bread dough can be just as satisfying and less difficult than pinching one's playmates. As children grow older and can be expected to know how to behave in normal situations, then meaningful consequences, enforced in a very matter-of-fact way, are often appropriate. Children who cannot be trusted to play without hurting others must clearly stay very near to an adult until they have learnt how to control their own behaviour sufficiently to manage without close adult support. Positive time out when a child spends time with a trusted adult doing a useful task such as preparing food for the whole class or mending something that was damaged in the rumpus and perhaps having time for quiet conversation about the problem can be very soothing. It is important that the adult is able to remain calm in the situation, though reflecting one's genuine sadness at a hurt that has happened is a true enough response.

There are also many occasions when a light touch is enough to avoid difficulties that the practitioner may see coming. Simply moving the adult's workplace to be beside the play can often calm a game that is becoming so rowdy that it is beginning to disrupt others. Gentle singing of a well-known rhyme can often help too. If the children can respond to the adults' actions, they have learnt to control the volume themselves without an adult having to say 'Quietly please', a phrase that can become so commonplace that the children come to ignore it. The gentle song, even in a very noisy room, does penetrate everyone's subconscious in a way that speech does not.

An adult response within the terms of the game is also generally successful. To go back to the example of the hairdressers who were holding the large log over the head of the child because it was, in their eyes, a hairdryer. The practitioner might judge that there is a safety issue here: the log is heavy, and the children involved a little unreliable. The adult might say, 'Put that log down, it is dangerous' and go across and take it away. The danger has been averted, but at the same time the bubble of play has also been destroyed. On the other hand, the adult might say, offering a basket of clothes pegs, 'It is time for the curling tongs now, let me put that hairdryer back into the storeroom.' Here the danger is averted and the play can continue.

The Steiner practitioner believes that an imaginative and sensitive word from the sidelines is often all that is needed to redirect play that becomes unhealthy or obsessive. Animal play in the room, for example, can become wild animal play and bring too much aggression and fear for the group to cope with. The common-sense response is that wild animals are only happy outside and not for indoor playtime. This will make sense to the children playing at tigers and jaguars especially if some tempting alternative is gently set before them. Tigers and jaguars do have to come indoors, of course, if they have hurt paws and need treatment from the vet. Seamlessly, the game is transformed from one of terrorising others to one of caring for those who are hurt. The adult might become the vet for a while to model how one cares for injured animals, and assistants will soon be bringing bandages and medicines to the surgery.

Creative discipline: longer-term responses

Once the immediate situation has been attended to, the Steiner practitioner knows that the power of the therapeutic story is often a great support to the child who is struggling socially and not able to play well. A short and simple story of a crab who found it hard to make friends needs no moral but will have a quiet effect on both the pincher and the pinched child. A more complex story in which archetypes of good and evil conflict, and the good is finally triumphant, such as many of the traditional fairy tales, may be what is needed in the case of the older child who is having difficulties in managing his or her own behaviour. Again, there will be benefit in the whole group hearing such a story.

A little of this active intervention at the start of the year with a new group can often lay sound foundations for play to unfold in safety and freedom. Knowing when the adult should step out of the children's play is as important as knowing when to step in. As long as they are safe and happy, this is their time to plan and carry out what they need to do. When a secure, relaxed atmosphere has been established, then children can be trusted in their own self-initiated play.

Key points

1. Self-initiated play, both indoors and out, is given a special place in the Steiner Waldorf early-childhood setting.
2. The Steiner practitioner sees this time as the appropriate time for free unconscious choice on the part of the child.
3. Play for the young child flows freely from one game to another with open-ended equipment and children changing roles with fluidity.

4. The child under five is often not aware of the division between play and the real world.
5. Steiner practitioners advocate that what children unconsciously choose to play and how they choose to play, meets the needs that they have and provides a tailor-made learning experience.
6. Lack of opportunity for free self-initiated play in childhood may lead to difficulties and weaknesses in adult life.
7. Unformed and flexible play equipment, both indoors and out, encourages flexibility, creativity and the learning of social skills.
8. The best accompaniment to support deep play in the children is the calm adult, actively and joyfully involved in meaningful work.
9. Safe play requires good social habits established and maintained by the practitioner.
10. Sensitivity for when intervention by the adult in play is necessary will come from knowledge of the children based on observation.

Reflections

The value of play

■ How important do you believe is the unguided self-initiated play of the young child, and what do you see as its main benefits?
■ How do you think that children learn to make good choices?
■ What value do you see for the practitioner in observing the child at play?

Supporting play

■ Do you believe that most children today have enough time and space to play?
■ What helps children to lose themselves in play and does this provide a worthwhile experience for them?
■ What do you believe the adults should be doing while the children are playing?

Equipment for play

■ Have you experienced children using toys and equipment originally in the service of the game?

- Have you experienced children's play being limited by a lack of flexibility in the equipment to which they have access?

Intervening in play

- What are the golden rules in your setting?
- How might you have intervened in the hairdressers game?

References

Clouder, C. and Nicol, J. (2008) *Creative Play for Your Toddler*, London: Gaia.

Jaffke, F. (2004) *On the Play of the Child: Indications by Rudolf Steiner for Working with Young Children*, Spring Valley, NY: WECAN.

Jenkinson, S. (2001) *The Genius of Play*, Stroud: Hawthorn Press.

Nicol, J. (2010) *Bringing the Steiner Waldorf Approach to Your Early Years Practice*, London: Routledge.

Oldfield, L. (2002) *Free to Learn*, Stroud: Hawthorn Press.

Steiner, R. (1996) *The Child's Changing Consciousness*, New York: Anthroposophic Press.

Tovey, H. (2007) *Playing Outdoors*, Maidenhead: Open University Press.

Winnicott, D. W. (1987) *The Child, the Family and the Outside World*, London: Pelican.

7 Rhythm and repetition

Introduction

In this chapter, the security and coherence offered by rhythm and the learning opportunities given by repetition are discussed in the context of the Steiner early-childhood setting. The idea of the breathing rhythm is introduced, and we explain how the young child learns through repetition in a spiral of development. Examples are given of the rhythmical and repeated routines for the day, the week and the year, through which young children can build trust in their environment and the adults caring for them there, including the value of the repeated story and of working with the seasons of the year, in songs, stories and activities. The celebration of festivals brings special highlights to the year, and we consider how this benefits the child and involves parents too.

Rhythm and repetition as key concepts

Rhythm and repetition stand alongside imitation and example as key concepts of Steiner Waldorf early-childhood education, and they will be reflected in the practice of any setting. Rhythm always brings order but not rigidity, form but not stultification. Repetition brings the opportunity for a deepening of understanding, whether it is of a well-loved story or a regular weekly walk.

All living things, from the simplest life form, work with rhythm and repetition, and it is this that makes complicated lives possible. The Steiner practitioner considers this is doubly so for young children who have the mission in their early years of trying to find coherence and meaning in

their lives. In Steiner settings, this task is supported by working with rhythm from tiny routines, such as a sequence for careful washing of the hands, through the rhythms of the day, the week and the year. Repeating these rhythms, large and small, brings a feeling of security to the children. They can experience how things go and know that their experience will be reinforced. Life is not random but held by the adults in a safe way.

The overarching rhythm of the year brings something more through its connection first with the seasons and second with an appropriate cycle of festivals. These provide the high points, prepared for, celebrated and tidied away, which will be repeated and developed each year. Festivals lift everyone out of day-to-day life and build connections with a much wider community. Careful choice of festivals and seasonal celebrations gives the young child a sense of being a small part in a global community.

The importance of rhythm

Steiner practitioners advocate that rhythm is a fundamental source of security for children. The fact that their coats hang in the same place today as they did yesterday, that the paints and brushes are arranged in the same way this week as they were last week on painting day, and that the lantern festival comes at the time of year when the daylight is decreasing, all help them to feel that their world can be depended upon. When children feel safe, they feel free enough to explore and to take risks.

> Children emphatically demand that they find ever again the order of things, thus signalling to adults how dependent they are on this experience. If those conditions exist, then the children can feel well and protected. If they do not exist, then the children can become restless and agitated. Any absence or disturbance of this order affects their feeling of well-being. It has an extraordinarily positive, even healing, effect on children when their daily activities are not chaotic but rather rhythmically organised, following a certain order every day
>
> (Patzlaff and Sassmannshausen 2007: 32).

Having rhythms in our lives helps us to feel connected to each other, to the natural world and even to the cosmos. Living things breathe and so live in a continual rhythm of in-breath and out-breath, receiving and giving until they stop and then cease to be alive. Breathing is not a rigid routine but responds to the needs of the body. If we are very active, we

breathe more quickly; if we are sitting quietly, we breathe slowly and deeply.

The rhythms and routines that are repeated in Steiner Waldorf early-childhood settings should be thought of in the same way, as responding to the needs of life. There is no need to stick to a rigid timetable. If needs be, the practitioner will speed things up a bit but then remember that the children need some quieter, deeper breathing in order to recuperate. When children are asked to contain themselves, to sit at the meal table or to gather quietly for story, this can be made easier for them by having each day follow the same rhythm, so they know what to expect and their bodies are accustomed to it. It is also easier for them if the practitioner ensures that an 'in-breath' of holding themselves contained is preceded and followed by an 'out-breath' of play, for example.

The value of repetition

Everyone who lives or works with young children knows of their need for repetition, not just of familiar rhythms of meals, playtimes and outings, but also of favourite rhymes, songs and stories. The general principle of repetition as a support to learning is also acknowledged in the way that the Steiner Waldorf setting is organised. Through repetition, children learn in a spiral of development. When they learn to walk, they try again and again to overcome gravity and pull themselves upright. Again and again they fall down, but they persevere until at last, through repetition, they master the next step. In the same way, when small children revel in hearing the same rhyme or story again and again, they are developing the inner pictures conjured up by the experience. They may hear the same words as yesterday, but, if there is no picture book, the illustrations that their imaginations paint for them in response to the words will change as they change.

That is why the practitioner may tell the same fairy tale to all the children in a mixed-age group, perhaps aged from rising three to nearly seven, and each child will have his or her own experience. The story may well be chosen to meet the needs of the oldest ones in the group who will appreciate the difficulties that the princess has to go through in order for evil to be defeated and good to triumph, as it does at the end of all true fairy tales. But, as the story is told calmly and steadily, the youngest child will not be harmed by frightening images, for example of the wicked witch that the princess meets, because the images that he or she makes

will be his or her own. Steiner practitioners do not put their own emotions into the telling of the story so that the children can make their own images, and these they will be able to cope with. The story will be repeated over days and perhaps weeks, and all the children's inner pictures will metamorphose day by day in those retellings as they unconsciously absorb different ideas from the story.

Creating a breathing rhythm for the day

By a breathing rhythm, we mean one that has the right balance between the times that draw the children in to be focused and attentive and the times for activities that encourage them to expand and be active. Here you might imagine the practitioner as the conductor of an orchestra skilfully and delicately holding together all the players and every bar of the music to make a harmonious whole. When this works well, everyone reaches the end of the session feeling satisfied and well nourished. Young children especially need a balanced rhythm to the waking part of their day, with its own harmonisation of in-breaths and out-breaths. In the Steiner Waldorf early-childhood centre, each group will have a suitable healthy daily rhythm, and, as Lynne Oldfield writes, 'The Rhythm soon becomes habit, and very quickly theses habits are established and become unquestioned, removing the need for instruction and direction' (2002: 72).

A typical daily rhythm

A typical morning session in a kindergarten with a mixed age range of three to rising seven might proceed as follows. The children arrive, hang up their coats and change into their indoor shoes or slippers. They come into the kindergarten room where the adults are already laying out the painting things. Some children see the familiar activity being prepared, put on their painting aprons and begin to help. When the table is all set for painting, they sit down to paint, as does at least one of the adults. When each child comes to a conclusion with their painting, he or she takes it to an adult, who will make sure that it is labelled with the child's name, and then the child will put it safely to dry and tidy up the painting things that have been used before going off for indoor play. As this is how the painting activity is conducted every week, there is no overt instruction needed.

Other children may have, of their own initiative, gone straight into playing on their arrival. They may be attracted by the painting session later when it is well under way and come to put on an apron and join in. Some children may be so busy with their play that the painting activity passes them by. The practitioner may choose to call the older children to come and paint while leaving the younger ones free to play. They will certainly be attracted to join in at some time, when they are quite ready in themselves.

When all the painters have finished and the activity is cleared away, then the adults go on to prepare the meal that comes in the middle of the morning. There is bread to slice and butter and fruit to chop. Some children are drawn to help with that, while others continue to play out of their own free will. Again the practitioner might call on the older children to help, for example to set the table ready for the snack. There will be plates and cups to count, place mats or napkins to set out and a centre-piece of flowers and perhaps a candle to be arranged.

Tidy-up time

When work is finished, the daily miracle of 'tidy-up time' begins. By now there has been much play, all the furniture has been moved about in the construction of a mighty castle and the play area is strewn with clothes, logs and other equipment that has been used in all the games.

Having packed away their own work in the food-preparation area, probably with some small helpers, the adults begin by starting to put the bigger pieces of furniture in their places and sorting equipment into piles. It may be part of the rhythm of this group to sing a simple tidy-up song at this point, but even if this is not done some children will be drawn to help while others play with renewed fervour as they realise that the end of playtime is fast approaching.

Now the experienced practitioner will work to draw in all the children to help with the tidying up. This could be done by making it part of a game (for example, truck drivers making deliveries) and by calling on the help of the oldest children in the group. The whole process is made easier when all the equipment has a proper 'home' to which it always returns. Knowing where everything goes and how it is stored is very empowering for the children, building their confidence both in the setting and in their lives generally. Through the power of imitation and example, rhythm and repetition, the daily miracle is achieved.

Personal care

When the physical care of the room is complete, perhaps finishing with some of the children sweeping the floor, all the children receive some physical care themselves. With appropriate adult support, each child will pay a visit to the toilet and then wash their hands. For practical reasons, this activity, and it is truly an activity full of learning possibilities, often overlaps with tidy-up time. In the overall rhythm of the session, it can be seen that after the big out-breath of self-initiated play, the children have gradually been drawn in through the tidying up. Now they will be supported with their personal hygiene.

The adults will make sure that the toilets are pleasant areas in which to spend time: carefully decorated, including natural decorations such as flowers and branches which change with the seasons and perhaps beautiful pictures. They will also encourage the children to take their time, to tuck in their clothes properly and will pay special attention to the care of hands with washing, drying and perhaps hand cream. In Steiner practice hands are an important symbol of humanness. With them we can achieve all kinds of practical things in the world – and we can reach out to each other. Some Steiner settings, especially those working with the youngest children, have the staff and facilities for each child to have his or her hands washed and dried by an adult. Others encourage the children to make a good job of it for themselves. Some settings provide individual soft cotton towels for each child as these give a much nicer sensory experience than paper towels and avoids the intrusive noise of the hot air blower while maintaining proper hygiene standards. As this personal care activity concludes, the children gather again in the main room of the setting, where the play has been. While they are gradually becoming ready for the next part of the rhythm of the day they might comb their hair, finding their own named comb or brush in its case in the basket where the combs or brushes live.

Ring time

Now the room is tidy and so are the children, and everyone is ready to move on to ring time. (See Appendix III for a sample ring time.) The children may be in need of some refreshment by now, even though it is not yet snack time, so fresh fruit slices or dried fruit and seeds are often shared at this point. Ring time is a combination of movement, music and words, generally in celebration of the time of year. The practitioner will put together a flowing sequence of poems, songs, finger games and whole-group games that is repeated for several days or weeks and that includes plenty of repetition within the sequence. This gives opportunities for variation (loudly/softly, quickly/slowly, for example) and well as allowing the children time to join in. Ring time will be learnt through imitation of the adults – not through instruction or direct teaching but through doing. The children will join in because it is enjoyable, because children love to move and to play with words and music and because it always happens at this time of day and in this way. It may always begin and end with the same verse or song.

Here there is a real contrast to the time of free play. Now the children are all doing the same thing at the same time and following the lead of the adult (see Fig. 7.1). Because they have had a good out-breath and have gradually been brought together into a group through tidy-up and toilet time, they are ready to spend fifteen or twenty minutes in this whole-group practitioner-led activity. At the beginning of the school year, when there are many new children, this in-breath of ring time may be shortened.

Snack time

Another hand wash, perhaps just a rinse this time, brings all to the snack table, which has been prepared earlier in the session. There may even have been a fine smell of soup or baking bread while ring time was going on, and the children are quickly settled in their places. The adults will settle themselves and put their hands to rest on the lap with a big gesture that the children will be drawn into. Then the candle can be lit, if that is the tradition in that kindergarten, and a blessing sung or spoken before the meal begins. Perhaps older children will be the 'waiters' carrying round the bowls of food to all the children as the adults dish up, or plates

Figure 7.1 Ring time.

of food will be carefully handed from hand to hand around the table. Snack time has a beginning, with a blessing, and an ending, with everyone taking hands and saying 'thank you for the meal'. It may be the habit to eat quietly, or this may be a time for conversation. The practitioner may even use this time to tell a little story that seems appropriate – stories of 'long ago when I was little' are often popular.

When the meal finishes, the dishes are collected and stacked and the chairs pushed in to the table or stacked at one side, most of the children will now go to get ready to go outside. A small team, perhaps of the older children, help to wash, dry and put away the crockery and cutlery and sweep under the table.

Outdoor time

Getting ready to go outside, like handwashing, is an activity in its own right not just something to be got through as quickly as possible. Steiner practitioners believe that whenever young children are supported to take care of their physical bodies, this shows them that they are worthy of respect and encourages them to learn to respect others as they grow up. When they see care modelled, the children build habits of caring for themselves, others and the world around them. So it is a serious task to prepare to move from indoors to outdoors. As outdoor play takes place in all weathers and often involves sand, water and mud, wet-weather gear, including waterproof trousers or dungarees, are essential for much of the school year. Putting these on is a major task to a three-year-old, and accomplishing this unaided is an achievement. Buttons, zips, buckles and bows all bring challenges and opportunities for helping each other and for learning from each other.

Keeping a sense of order in the cloakroom or lobby areas is also important to the Steiner practitioner. This part of the kindergarten is designed so that the children are able to keep order there themselves with plenty of accessible pegs and shelves for hats and gloves and space for slippers, boots and shoes. Enough space is needed for the children to dress and undress themselves, and if cloakroom space is short then some do this in the kindergarten room. The sensible practitioner adds large loops to the outdoor clothes to make it easier for children to hang them up and provides pegs to keep boots and slippers in pairs.

Now is the time for a good out-breath in the fresh air. Here again the adults will have tasks to undertake, looking after the garden and play areas and, in fine weather, bringing out indoor cleaning, mending and food-preparation tasks that are portable and suitable for outside. The children are free to play and move about as they wish, remembering the golden rule that 'we take care of each other'. There will probably be paths to run along, trees, logs or other play equipment to climb on, sand and mud areas to dig. Some may choose to help the adults who are sweeping or gardening or mending the indoor play frame that has become wobbly with use.

It is important that this is not just a ten-minute run around. The children need time to relax into their outdoor play in the same way as they did indoors, although the nature of outdoor play is different. Some kindergartens have found that the way to prevent this vital outside time from being shortened is to put it at the beginning of the kindergarten session when the children arrive in the morning.

Towards the end of the outdoor time, the children need a signal that it will soon be time to come in, and this is usually the beginning of a tidy-up of the outdoor equipment. Sand boxes must be covered and tools put away, then the children come in and prepare themselves for story time, leaving tidy the outdoor clothes that they have taken off and washing their hands.

Story time and the end of the session

In the kindergarten room, preparations will have been made for story time, probably by the children who helped to clear away after the snack. This means that the children come inside to a familiar arrangement of chairs arranged in a semicircle around the practitioner's 'story chair'. This is a quiet time, a contrast to outdoor playtime, and the reliable use of rhythm means that the children become used to this transition and usually settle easily into the appropriate mood to receive the story.

In most Steiner Waldorf early-childhood settings, stories are learned by heart by the practitioner and told to the children. There is no book, no showing of pictures between the adult and the listeners. There will be a familiar start to the story routine, perhaps a candle will be lit, simple soft music played or a song sung, then the telling of the story will begin. It will be told in a simple non-dramatic way so that the children can take it in as they need to without the adult imposing any emotional content in the delivery of the tale. The same story will be repeated for at least a week. At the end of the story there will be a familiar ending, maybe a song, music and a verse spoken (the same every day) which eases the children back from their immersion in the world of the story and signals that it is time to prepare to go home, or perhaps to the setting's afternoon care provision.

The end has now been reached to a typical Steiner kindergarten morning session. The rhythm has been healthy for the children with its alternation of activities that draw the child out and activities that bring a quieter and more inward mood. As the daily rhythm repeats day after day so the children feel secure in knowing what will happen next and how it will happen, so they learn to trust that the world is coherent and meaningful and manageable.

Stories and storytelling

Steiner practitioners tell 'house and garden' stories. This means stories that young children will recognise as part of their familiar world, stories about what happens at home and in the world close to home, stories about things that might happen today, tomorrow or any time soon. There are nature stories that allow the child to imagine how the natural world works, how the seeds are taken down under the earth in the autumn to safe, warm beds where the winter cold will not harm them and how the woodland creatures welcome the spring with such joy after the long winter rest.

Steiner practitioners also tell traditional fairy stories. These are especially suitable for the older children in the kindergarten, the five- and six-year-olds, and help to answer the deep questions that are beginning to occur to them as they wake up to their new capacities. In every true fairy tale there are difficulties, even difficulties that seem to be impossible to overcome, but in the end Good is triumphant and Evil is defeated, hearts' desires are achieved and wickedness is punished. This is the message that children want and need to hear, not because they will never encounter difficult and bad things in their lives but precisely because they will, and they need to know that there are many mysterious ways in which they can be transformed. There is always the hope of a good outcome in the end no matter how difficult things may seem on the way there. Fairy stories give children very positive and empowering messages. Such stories exist in all cultures throughout the world, and the practitioner has a wealth of alternatives from which to select something that seems to suit the moment.

Rudolf Meyer writes about the importance of fairy stories for children: 'Bringing alive the many different moods in the telling or artistic presentation of fairy tales stimulates the powers of listening and feeling in the soul; and this is one useful way of developing concentration in children who flitter from one impression to the next' (1988: 181).

By telling the story rather than reading it, the practitioner shows that the story is worthwhile and has value enough to be learnt. It will also be repeated over at least a week and maybe for three weeks to give time for it to become a well-loved friend. There is also no barrier between the teller and the listener. There are no pictures and nothing in the practitioner's voice to curtail the children's freedom to make of the story what they will, to build in their imagination the pictures that they need. This enables a long story full of rich images to be told in a mixed-age-range kindergarten. The six-year-olds will be well fed by all this richness, and the three-year-olds will take from it what they need and can cope with.

Working with the week

Daily rhythms are not the only ones to be found in the Steiner Waldorf early-childhood setting. There will also be a rhythm of the week. For the children the days of the week are often characterised by what food will be prepared and served: rice day, bread day and soup day, for example. Many settings work with a rhythm of serving a different grain on each day of the week in a regular rhythm. In Britain, our diet is often strongly based on wheat, but there are grains popular in other parts of the world that bring different qualities, and the snack menu is an opportunity to introduce some of these to the children.

There will also be other rhythms to the week, for example different activities on regular days: Monday is painting day, Tuesday is soup-making day, Wednesday is bread-making day, Thursday is walk day and Friday is home care day. Many settings now have one day a week on which more time is spent outside and longer walks are taken – to a natural setting such as a nature reserve or country park if possible.

Some settings have an eurythmist who visits once a week. This is a teacher with a special training in the movement art known as eurythmy, which builds on the connections between speech or music and move-ment. As this only happens once a week it will be repeated over many weeks so that the children can follow and join in with the movement routines simply though imitation.

The seasonal rhythm of the year and the cycle of the festivals

The seasonal cycle of the year is one that young children naturally respond to. Wherever they live, town or country, they are in tune with the seasons. Helle Hackmann expresses it as follows:

Nature makes frames around us, and it makes a big difference as to where we are in the course of the year. Each time has its own quality and each season makes us remember the previous one and look forward to the next one. Nature helps us remember prior experiences and build joy for the upcoming ones.

(Heckmann 2011: 10)

These seasonal themes are reflected in the decoration of the setting: appropriate flowers, branches, etc., in the ring-time material, and sometimes in the story time too. There may be seasonally appropriate crafts as part of the weekly rhythm or as additional activities when the daily activity is finished. These could be simple things such as making garlands of autumnal leaves and seeds, or paper butterflies in the early summer, to decorate the room. (See Appendix II.)

In addition to this acknowledgement of the seasons of the year, there will also be a cycle of festivals celebrated in the setting. Every human civilisation celebrates festivals with their essential ingredients of symbolism, ritual and joy. As Marjorie Thatcher writes: 'A living celebration of festivals is one of the most important gifts we can give our children' (Thatcher 2011: 4).

The practitioner will chose those which mean something to her and to the families of the group. In practice in Britain this often means that there is a framework of Christian festivals, with others included that are significant to the families of the settings, and the practitioner will often involve parents in the preparation and celebration of these much-loved events.

When celebrating festivals it is important that there is a time of preparation, a special celebration day and then a time in which the festival fades slowly away – for example, in January, there may still be Christmas songs and stories which the children heartily enjoy long after all the decorations at home have been packed away. Because Steiner settings normally have an age range that spans more than one year band (three through to turning seven-year-olds), there is an opportunity for the child to encounter the round of the year in the setting more than once. All practitioners recognise the joy with which a familiar poem, seasonal activity or festival event is greeted for the second or third time. Here is a chance for children to experience that this year they are able to achieve something that they could not a year ago and even to be able to help the younger ones coming to it for the first time. So, through rhythm and repetition, children experience that they are growing more skilful, taller and more able to make a difference in their own small world.

Key points

1. The Steiner practitioner sees rhythm as a fundamental source of security for the young child who is trying to make sense of the world.
2. Rhythm breathes in a pulse of contracting in-breaths, such as coming together for story, and relaxing out-breaths, such as free playtime.

3. Repetition enables young children to learn skills in a spiralling progression of development.
4. Repetition of a story told without a picture book allows the children to make the pictures in their imaginations that they need to.
5. A daily rhythm with appropriate arrangements of out-breaths and in-breaths will help the day to flow smoothly with little need for instruction.
6. A weekly rhythm will be marked by the regular appearance of activities and by the snack menu.
7. The seasons provide an important rhythm to the year for the young child, which is reflected in decoration, activities, songs, poems and stories in the Steiner setting.
8. This yearly rhythm is deepened by the celebration of a yearly cycle of festivals, appropriate to the location of the setting and cultural background of the families that attend.
9. Parents will usually be involved in the celebration of festivals.
10. All the festivals celebrated in the kindergarten need a time of preparation, the celebration itself and a time to fade away afterwards.

Reflections

The value of rhythm and repetition

■ How do you see rhythm and repetition supporting the young child's sense of security and his ability to learn?
■ Do you see children choosing repetition, for example of stories and songs?
■ Do you see children learning through repetition?

Working with a healthy rhythm

■ Can you see a healthy rhythm of in- and out-breaths in your own setting?
■ Can you see examples of an unhealthy rhythm that does not support the children?
■ What advantages and disadvantages can you see in the practitioner learning to tell stories by heart and not using picture books?

The rhythm of the year

- How do you experience that children are affected by the seasons?
- What cycle of festivals is celebrated in your setting?
- What do you think are the essentials of a festival celebration in your setting?

References

Heckmann, H. (2011) 'The Rhythm of Life', in N. Foster (ed.), *The Seasonal Festivals in Early Childhood: Seeking the Universally Human*, New York: WECAN Publications, pp. 9–10.

Meyer, R. (1988) *The Wisdom of Fairy Tales*, Edinburgh: Floris Books.

Oldfield, L. (2002) *Free to Learn*, Stroud: Hawthorn Press.

Patzlaff, R. and Sassmannshausen, W. (eds.) (2007) *Developmental Signatures: Core Values and Practices in Waldorf Education for Children 3–9*. New York: AWSNA.

Thatcher, M. (2011) 'Festivals for Young Children and the Cycle of the Year', in N. Foster (ed.), *The Seasonal Festivals in Early Childhood: Seeking the Universally Human*, New York: WECAN Publications, pp. 3–4.

Wilson, F. R. (1998) *The Hand*, New York: Vintage Books.

8 Domestic and artistic activities

Introduction

In this chapter we shall consider first of all why domestic work is included so regularly and thoroughly in Steiner early-childhood settings and also why such emphasis is given to artistic and craft work both for the children and the adults caring for them. We shall describe how enthusiasm, dexterity and understanding of the world are developed by such a curriculum and how the development of both adults' and children's creativity is seen as such an essential component of Steiner education.

The importance of domestic and artistic activities

Domestic and artistic activities have an important place in the rhythm of the day and of the week, and both the practical and the artistic feature strongly throughout the Steiner Waldorf curriculum up to the school leaving age. Indeed, all the initial teacher-education courses include a substantial component of artistic work for the self-development of the student as well as pedagogical artistic work such as toy- and puppet-making. Teachers' conferences and continuing professional development sessions will normally include some art-based sessions, and in most schools and settings there will be an artistic activity as part of the staff meeting. This indicates the importance given to artistic education and development within the Steiner movement for children and for adults. Couple this emphasis with the obvious joy that young children find in creative expression it is hardly surprising that you will find 'arts and crafts' figuring regularly in the curriculum of the Steiner Waldorf early-childhood setting.

It may be more surprising to find the emphasis that is given to domestic work or 'the art of living' as it is sometimes described. You will see children involved in food preparation, washing up and all kinds of housework and also working outdoors, gardening and doing wood-work, for example. Even if the children are busy playing and not actually taking part, or that activity is not particularly appropriate for children to join, you will see adults undertaking all kinds of indoor and outdoor tasks that you might imagine should be done after the children have gone home. There may be an ironing board set up in the kindergarten and an adult engaged in unfolding, spraying, ironing and hanging up laundry such as table napkins, aprons and cloths that have been used in the kindergarten. In the garden you might see the practitioner pruning the trees and bushes or chopping firewood while the children are playing outdoors.

Domestic activities: involving the child in what needs to be done

Steiner practice places great emphasis on children preparing for and washing up after their own meals and being involved in the care and maintenance of their own environment. Fine and gross motor skills are developed through this kind of work. In a Steiner setting you may see children doing such things as spreading bread, rolling pastry or washing fruit ready for a meal. Outside they may be sowing seeds in the spring time or sanding wooden toys and testing the smoothness of their work on their fingertips and their cheeks. There are so many ways in which fine motor skills can be developed not by specially designed educational equipment but by everyday activities. There are just as many oppor-tunities for the development of gross motor skills. Turning the handle of a grain mill or sawing wood with a small bow saw are activities that involve the whole body. The same is true of using a broom to sweep the floor, an action that also crosses the body and thus helps to build inte-gration and coordination for a child's movements. Many settings prepare vegetable soup once a week, which involves scrubbing, washing, peeling and chopping the vegetables that go into it. As this is done every week, and always on the same day, the children will be used to handling the equipment needed. Aprons will be put on, scrubbing brushes wielded, peelers manipulated and sharp knives used with care and attention. Clearly appropriate care needs to be taken that such things as knives and peelers are well supervised, but from the age of three or four their proper use is well within the capabilities of almost all children. Using potentially dangerous equipment such as knives in a carefully overseen situation encourages a special attitude on the part of the children. They are aware that they must use their tools properly as they are potentially dangerous, yet the regular repetition of this activity makes them quite comfortable with it.

The soup preparation also shows to the children how much can be achieved by working as a group, so this is a social experience as well. This is the case with many of the domestic tasks – many hands make light work when you are chopping vegetables or polishing windows, digging potatoes or pegging out laundry. Some children will be much more enthusiastic about a particular task than others. However, all the children will see the work that is needed to feed the class and take care of their surroundings, and this is a valuable lesson that does not need to be spelled out verbally but can be quietly absorbed as the same tasks are repeated day after day and week after week. The interest of individual children will ebb and flow, but the practitioner will be aware of each child's engagement and proficiency and progress over the time they are in the group (perhaps two or three or even four years). When the children reach five or six years of age, then the practitioner may decide that the time has come to insist on their participation if it should appear they are deliberately avoiding a certain task. Or the practitioner may find another task for them that tests the same kind of skills.

Learning about the world

Cooking is chemistry in another guise, and the kinds of activities that have been described are teaching the children, again in a way that is not emphasised or even necessarily verbalised, how the world works. In Steiner settings the children see and begin to understand how human intervention, for example, makes a carrot out of a tiny seed and a patch of earth, or how a fire is lit. They also learn that fires are hot and that care must be taken around them – there are rules that must be followed for the safety of all. That fire can be used to cook food – popcorn or potatoes, for example – as well as to warm cold fingers and toes in the winter.

Freya Jaffke discusses the importance that orderly work in the presence of young children has in supporting their understanding of and trust in the world and gives the following list of points that such activity should embody:

- Creating clear work processes into which the children can be integrated very easily. In accordance with their age, the children may occasionally turn the work into a game but they are still finding their place in the work of adults.
- Thinking through the work in advance and carrying it out in a logical order, up to and including tidying up the workplace.
- Working calmly and briskly, though not hectically, without boredom and always with pleasure. Thoughts should be concentrated fully on the adults' own activity as well as being extended over what is happening in the room so that all the children feel that they are being taken care of.
- Persevering in our work over a period of at least several days (with exceptions, of course). In this way we repeat our work regularly and do not simply do it when we happen to think of it or spontaneously feel like it.

Jaffke suggests that when this happens, 'The children are left in peace – paradoxical as that may sound – and do not constantly need to ask "What are you doing today" or "What are we doing now?"' (2002: 41).

Domestic work gives good opportunities for problem-solving too. How can things be pegged onto the high washing line or the top windows polished? Something stable is needed to climb up on. How can the wet washing be taken to the line without making the floor very wet? It needs to be wrung out and carried in a bucket not a basket.

All young children are trying to find coherence and meaningfulness in their daily life, and this is well supported by these kinds of discoveries. There are also many opportunities for the children to make discoveries about the uses of literacy and numeracy too. Jars of jam have to be labelled and recipes have to be read by the adult. The children will themselves be involved in numerical discoveries. The correct number of cups, bowls and spoons need to be put on the table. The apple needs to be divided into the correct number of pieces so that everyone may have one. Sometimes scales and measuring jugs are used, and all the time this is in response to the needs of daily life not as an exercise contrived to test a specific skill or teach a specific point.

Domestic work in the kindergarten is an impulse to play, as conveyed in the following example:

Being involved with the domestic activities in the kindergarten also stimulates play at this age, and joining the adult in the washing of the dolls' clothes, for instance, often leads to extended play; in creating the right place to hang the washing, by stringing lines across the garden, fetching washing baskets to hang it up, and building a little house nearby with screens and muslins to extend the 'home' play, which could (and has in my kindergarten) led to all the children becoming involved in the process of doing the washing, hanging it up, making ironing boards out of planks with wooden blocks as irons, dressing the dolls, cooking the dinner and generally involving all and sundry in household activities [see Fig. 8.1].

(Nicol 2010: 25)

Developing lifelong attitudes

By helping to feed and care for themselves, the Steiner practitioner believes that children are unconsciously learning a self-resilience that will remain with them for life, as well as useful domestic skills. They see that such things are possible and manageable. In fact there is much more of an emphasis on food preparation and housework in many Steiner Waldorf settings in recent years as such things are, perhaps, less likely to be part

Figure 8.1 Washing up.

of a child's experience in the home environment. Many practitioners see this as a way of balancing out the child's experiences. There are all kinds of very good reasons why children's family homes may no longer be able to provide some of the 'hands on' experiences of homemaking that children can be involved in, but their childcare setting can fill these gaps.

All domestic work shows caring for the world in some very tangible way. Dusting, polishing and sweeping, for example, are gestures of 'stroking the world', which may teach children far more respect and care for the earth than all the intellectual teaching of environmental education that they receive later. The attitudes, habits and views of the world acquired before the age of seven really do stay into adulthood and are hard to change. It is Steiner practitioners' view that young children who have been involved in food preparation would be more likely to take a healthy interest in how their food is prepared as an adult. As young children, they see a 'home' setting being kept clean and beautiful and carry away with them this picture of how homes could be with an inclination to find the same qualities in their future homes. The small gestures of care for the environment – not wasting food, looking after and mending things, gardening – add up to a respect for the environment.

Experiencing life in Steiner settings should also show children that there is joy to be found in the tasks that have to be repeated time and time again, such as washing up. Young children actually do love these kind of tasks both because of the sensory experiences involved (warm bubbly water) and because they love to do real work with adults and to make a difference to the world. To see the dirty dishes cleaned, dried and put back on the shelf ready for the next meal is satisfying and comforting for them – there will be more meals in the future. If the adults do their work happily and enthusiastically, then children will find and keep a natural love for useful work themselves.

It is very important that the adults in the Steiner setting do not see their home care tasks as drudgery, because children imitate inner moods as well as outer actions. The practitioner and other adults in the setting will bring enthusiasm again and again to those tasks that have to be repeated time after time. Is not the washing up an opportunity to enjoy the company of those who are working with you? Many practitioners save this task for their older pupils who particularly relish a chance to chat with their teacher. The adult working in the Steiner setting cultivates joy in doing all the jobs that are necessary to run the 'home' and see them as opportunities to show the children that there is pleasure to be found in them all.

Indoor and outdoor tasks

The range of tasks, indoors and outdoors, in which the children participate is wide. Preparing food can include scrubbing, chopping, slicing,
peeling, measuring, weighing, stirring, grinding, grating, kneading,
shaping, carrying, rolling out, cutting out, greasing, sieving, counting,
squeezing, snipping and arranging, with the wealth of fine and large
motor movements that these will involve. Clearing away after the meal
will often include folding napkins, sorting laundry, scraping and stack-
ing plates and bowls, collecting spoons, wiping the table and sweeping
the floor as well as washing and drying up and putting everything away.
Toys and furniture will need to be dusted, cleaned, polished or oiled and
sometimes mended. Windows will need to be cleaned and plants will
need to be watered. Laundry will need to be washed, wrung out, hung
up, taken in, folded and ironed. Many of these tasks can be taken outdoors to do, in fine weather at least, and some settings have a covered
area out of doors where such things can be done in all weathers.

There are also the usual outdoor tasks. In addition to gardening work
through the seasons, there are always paths to sweep, outdoor toys and
equipment to care for, the compost to take care of and the feeding of the
birds to attend to. The outdoors is also a good place to invite special
visitors from time to time, such as the basket maker or the wood carver,
if the setting is lucky enough to have contact with these people. There is
seasonal work such as processing a sheaf of wheat or apple-pressing in
the autumn, storing vegetables, making wreaths for Christmas, collecting and cutting wood to building warming fires in very cold weather or
for special cooking, spring-cleaning tasks such as carrying out large
pieces of furniture to clean, washing the curtains in fine weather and
cleaning out the garden shed. (See Appendix II.)

In a typical Steiner setting there is, of course, more to do than time
allows, so the experienced practitioner will prioritise on the basis of the
perceived needs of the children and the practicalities of the situation.
There may be children in the group who would benefit from either fine or
large motor-skills development or who have something to learn from a
task that will involve working closely together, or there may be a child
who needs the opportunity of a quiet job one to one with an adult. The
practitioner will bear in mind such things as the age of the children, the
number of adults, the space to work indoors or outside, the availability of
hot water and other practical matters, including the weather. Rudolf

Steiner himself, even before the first kindergarten was founded, made clear statements about the importance of this kind of work for young children:

> The task of the kindergarten teacher is to adjust work taken from daily life so that it becomes suitable for the children's play activities . . . Whatever a young child is told to do should not be artificially contrived by adults who are comfortable in our intellectual culture, but should spring from life's ordinary tasks. The whole point of a [kindergarten] class is to give young children the opportunity to imitate life in a simple and wholesome way.
>
> (Steiner 1996: 81)

Artistic and craft activities

In a Steiner kindergarten the range of possibilities for artistic and craft activities is very broad. There will be an artistic component of speech, song and movement during the daily ring time, and songs and sometimes musical instruments will be used at other times during each day as well. There will be storytelling every day and sometimes puppetry. During each week and alongside the domestic rhythm of activities there will be artistic activities such as painting, drawing, eurythmy and modelling. In addition there will be craft work, often related to the season or the festival rhythm throughout the year. Crafts may include making kites in the windy autumn days, making lanterns as the days get shorter, making Christmas decorations and gifts, bird feeders around Valentine's day, pom-pom chicks or hares at Easter, making paper butterflies, May crowns with ribbons, midsummer posies and folders for all the paintings at the end of the school year. Included will be the skills of sewing, threading, knotting, measuring, cutting, teasing, carding, felting, finger knitting, plaiting, folding, gluing, tying, sanding and many others.

Some of these activities will involve every child, some will be open to whichever children are drawn to come to them, and some will be done by the practitioner or another adult, in the presence of the children. There may also be some special artistic and craft projects which are just for the older children in the group, such as a special drawing book or a doll-making project. Again the practitioner will plan from observing the children in the group and taking into account the practicalities of the setting and its resources.

The importance of the arts to young children

Steiner teachers and practitioners all acknowledge art to be important in education, including teacher education, and Steiner education gives it a particular emphasis both for children and for adults. Rudolf Steiner himself said:

> Children need art – both fine arts and poetry and music. And there is a way of being actively engaged in both sorts that is suitable for children in their school years. If you are a teacher you should not talk too much about one or another art form being 'useful' for the training of certain human faculties. After all, art exists for its own sake. Teachers should love art so much that they do not want this experience to be lost to children. They will then see how the children grow through their experiences in art. It is art that awakens their intelligence to full life.
>
> (Quoted in Juenemann and Weitmann 1994)

The actions involved develop fine and large motor skills, focus, perseverance and many other attributes (see Fig. 8.2). These can also be covered in the domestic activities already described, but artistic activities also provide opportunities for creativity and individual freedom.

As discussed in Chapters 6 and 7, in Steiner practice conscious individual choice is kept to a minimum for children under seven years of age. The aim is to keep the children unconscious about what they do so that they can drift dreamily from one part of the session to the next, carried by rhythm and very familiar repeated songs and phrases. Children enter the Steiner kindergarten room at the beginning of the session and are not asked, 'Do you want to help with the bread-making, or would you like to play or join in with the craft activity today?' Instead, the bread-making is just there for them to be drawn to if it happens, the play equipment is also there, and the craft work will be got out once the bread-making things are tidied away. Instead of making a conscious choice for one thing, and consequently against another, children go where they are unconsciously drawn, either by the appeal of the activity or by the companions already involved, or by the rhythmical habits that they have developed during their time in the setting. Steiner practitioners believe that if children are free to go where they are inclined and do not have to make a decision, this is real freedom for them.

As explained in Chapter 6, when children go into self-initiated play, they are again in a free space, a boundaried and safe space, in which they

Figure 8.2 Finger knitting.

can play out what they need to. Anything artistic has this element of real freedom, which is freedom of expression. When children face the space in which they usually play and are ready to play, they face a free space which they can fill with what comes out of them. In the same way, when they collect their blank painting paper and their paints, they have a free space to fill. The same is true when they are given a piece of modelling material such as beeswax. The practitioner does not circumscribe the artistic activity by giving a pre-printed paper which has to be painted in or even a topic such as rainbows and does not usually say that today, for example, we are all going to model mice. Sometimes a story may be given as an introduction to an activity which the practitioner will follow by painting or modelling something from the story that the children may choose, unconsciously, to imitate. But the freedom to create comes out of the child through the inspiration of imitation.

The following description of painting in the kindergarten gives an impression of how the children's freedom is protected and nurtured by artistic activity:

> Painting, to start with, is therefore an occupation similar to the other communal activities of baking, washing, clearing up and all the other things that have their

set place in the rhythm of the week. A considerable time is spent in preparation, with the putting on of aprons, and the giving out of paint boards, paper, brushes and paint pots. The children must be encouraged to do as much as possible for themselves. The kindergarten teacher endeavours to put the experiencing of colour in the very centre . . . What the children then do with their brush, paper and flowing colours is left to themselves. However, the kindergarten teacher also sits in front of her own painting board and carefully and joyfully lays on beautiful surfaces of red and yellow.

(Juenemann and Weitmann 1994: 37)

Seasonal craft activities

In a Steiner setting, a seasonal craft activity such as making paper butter-flies may be more prescribed by the materials available, tissue paper and pipe cleaners, for example. Usually the sight of an adult engaged in this work, or even just getting out the materials for it, will bring a flurry of children wanting to do just the same thing. But there is always the possibility of using these materials to make something quite different. The butterflies often get some paper flowers to visit and are sometimes joined by dragonflies and bees, or by much stranger and more fanciful creatures. Sometimes the practitioner will settle down to make a puppet, for example, and the children who gather around will find that there is a box of felt scraps and the sewing equipment that they need to create what they wish to, at the same time as the adult is working. The adult has time to encourage and help the children in their project, but a lot will be left to their own initiative. They may come up against a problem or a difficulty and not find a way to overcome it. Even their friends' help may not be enough. The adult will then decide whether to give them more help so that they finish what they have started, or whether, especially with children of four or younger, they should be allowed to just drift away into play and their unfinished project recycled into something else.

The importance of artistic practice for adults

Artistic work plays a large part in all training programmes for Steiner early-childhood staff, and artistic practice plays a part in ongoing teacher development. This artistic work will include the skills that the practi-tioner needs to make equipment for the setting, perhaps seasonal paint-ings or felt wall hangings, puppets and scenery for a puppet play, or maybe words and music for a ring time, or a specially written story for the class. It will also include artistic experiences for adult self-development, such as singing, drama, modelling and eurythmy, which are not directly related to working with young children. The following helps to put this emphasis in its place in Steiner teacher education:

> Children are born artists. They joyfully engage in activities, employing their creative faculties and stand so-to-say in the midst of life through their active work. They enter into the essence of things unconsciously, while we adults are rather more onlookers, observers and critics, keeping our distance . . . The art of education consists of leading young human beings into a conscious understanding of the world without losing their creative potential or individual formative powers. This needs time. All kinds of artistic activities are invaluable, as long as the adults are willing to become artists themselves.
>
> (Patzlaff and Sassmannshausen 2007: 108)

When we do something artistic, just like the children, we use our individual creativity. We can honestly say that teaching is an art. The Steiner practitioner plans time with the children and also has to respond in the moment to what happens when with them. This planning and the 'in the moment' responses come from the same well of individual creativity that are used when one paints, draws, sings, etc. It is not a matter of referring to a book but of bringing something out of our own being and making it manifest outside ourselves. This is an expression of our individuality, our own personal way of giving to the world something unique that was not there before, whether it is a painting or a story or a verbal communication that helps a situation in the class.

Artistic work can be seen as a vent for emotional states, but it is also a statement of something essentially human and not part of the life of animals. A human being might take something from nature, such as a piece of wood, and create a unique cultural article, such as a model of a child's head or a musical instrument. Inner capacities have transformed something into something else. Or an adult might make a comment that supports a child in a difficult situation, or supports the group of children to develop a good habit. This is just as creative and just as artistic. The more that we practise being artists, the more able we become to act artistically as practitioners. This is the reason that art is so important in initial teacher education and in continuing teacher development.

Key points

1. Both artistic and domestic activities appear regularly in the Steiner early-childhood setting.
2. Everyday domestic activities develop both fine and gross motor skills.
3. Orderly work in the presence of young children supports their understanding of and trust in the world.
4. Domestic work can be a good impulse to play.
5. Through looking after themselves and their environment, children learn self-resilience, satisfaction in work and respect for their environment.
6. Like play, artistic activity encourages creativity and real freedom.
7. The activities are available and the children are drawn to join them out of their unconscious interest.
8. Within the artistic activities there will be opportunities for the children's artistic freedom to flourish.
9. Artistic work is also seen as an important component of teacher education, both initially and as part of ongoing development.
10. By fostering artistic activity for ourselves as adults, we nurture our creativity and ability to respond 'in the moment' to children's needs.

Reflections

Domestic activity with children

- What advantages and disadvantages can you see in children being involved in domestic work?
- How do you or could you involve children in domestic activities in your setting?
- Select a domestic task and consider the learning opportunities in it for young children.

Artistic activity with the children

- How does your setting provide opportunities for artistic freedom for the children?
- What are the advantages and disadvantages of leaving children free to come to activities out of their own unconscious choices?

Artistic activity for the practitioner

■ How is the practitioner strengthened by artistic practice as part of initial and ongoing teacher education?
■ What type of artistic activity do you feel might strengthen your practice?

References

Jaffke, F. (2002) *Work and Play in Early Childhood*, Edinburgh: Floris Books.

Juenemann, M. and Weitmann, F. (1994) *Drawing and Painting in Rudolf Steiner Schools*, Stroud: Hawthorn Press.

Nicol, J. (2010) *Bringing the Steiner Waldorf Approach to Your Early Years Practice*, 2nd edn, London: Routeledge.

Patzlaff, R. and Sassmannshausen, W. (eds.) (2007) *Developmental Signatures: Core Values and Practices in Waldorf Education for Children 3–9*. New York: AWSNA.

Steiner, R. (1996) *The Child's Changing Consciousness and Waldorf Education*, London: Rudolf Steiner Press.

9 Observation and assessment

Introduction

In this chapter we explore what kind of observational practice is most supportive in the ongoing efforts to solve the riddle of the individual child. We discuss the concept of objective observation and how the Steiner Waldorf practitioner tries to develop this faculty through exercises. Children at play, when that play comes from their own initiative and is not guided by the adult, are especially worthy of careful observation. We will look at how this observation might be done, and at what might lead to a deeper understanding of what children really needs from us. This deeper task, usually done with colleagues, is called child study and is a particular feature of the work of the Steiner Waldorf practitioners. We show how both formative and summative assessment is used in the Steiner Waldorf setting and how the practitioner adapts to working with current regulations.

The child as a riddle

Rudolf Steiner described the child as a riddle that the practitioner or teacher works constantly to solve. This is a useful analogy in that it reminds us that understanding children takes effort and is never a finished task as the child changes all the time, and so do we. How does the practitioner learn about children? Theories of child development can be studied, and this is important in giving us frameworks for understanding, but observation of children is necessary in order to fill out these theoretical structures. First we take an interest in children, a warm interest that gives us knowledge about them, and then we want to turn that knowledge into skills. As Rudolf Steiner writes in his significant essay 'The Education of the Child' (also known as 'Educating Children Today') 'The child who lives in such an atmosphere of love and warmth and who has around him really good examples for his imitation, is living in his proper element' (2008: 38). This warm interest is a foundation of the reflective practice of the Steiner Waldorf practitioner.

To become proficient in the skills of supporting and nurturing children in their development requires not only outer actions but also inner work on one's own self-development. Developing equanimity and an unprejudiced view of the world helps the practitioner to have objective clarity and intuitive grasp and gives a source of inspiration. First we observe, next we search for the words to create a clear picture of what we have perceived, then our behaviour with the child can become a reflection of our perceptions. Observation and the words that are used are both an important influence on the adult's activity with the child.

In Steiner Waldorf education there is a common practice throughout settings and schools of making a detailed observation of a child and building it into a word picture that is as accurate as possible. This is followed by an attempt to look at that picture and make some deeper statements about the child. Out of those statements may come some suggestions for next steps for those who work with the child. This is done with colleagues and sometimes with parents and is the activity known as child study and forms a regular part of the pedagogical study that colleagues do together. The practice of making assessments of a child's progress and recording them on a profile sheet is also common in Steiner early-childhood settings and is seen as a valuable tool.

Practising objective observation

There is a proverbial German story that goes as follows. A man found that his axe was missing and he immediately suspected his neighbour's son. After all, the boy looked like a thief, walked like a thief and talked like a thief. Then the man found his axe lying where he had left it. The next time he saw his neighbour's son, he looked just like any other honest boy. Observation by human beings cannot help but be subjective, and assumptions and experiences colour how we see things, but we can at least try to keep our observations objective. How do we recognise when an observation is less than objective? An observation is attached to a particular moment of a child's biography but it can be framed by previous experiences of that child. 'She always reacts like that when someone interrupts her game', is not an objective observation. The assumptions that the observer already had about the child may easily have coloured what was seen. A pattern of behaviour may have been seen just because the observer expected to see it. But it did not actually happen like that this time.

The crucial things about observation that the Steiner practitioner strives for is to be as objective as possible. This includes not only endeavouring to prevent the past clouding the present, it also involves keeping a close watch on the language that is used to record observations. Terms with negative connotations can so easily creep in, terms such as 'bossy' instead of 'this child appears to enjoy controlling play', or 'rough and unkind' when what is meant is 'careless in physically handling others'. It is also equally possible to err in the direction of sentimentality. What is meant when a girl is described as 'sweet' or 'delightful'? Practice in techniques of objective observation is part of the initial teacher-education programme for Steiner Waldorf practitioners and teachers. One exercise often suggested is to find a characteristic in a person and then also to look to find the opposite there too. This can be practised by looking at a portrait. We might say that the person portrayed looks strong and confident, but then can we find something vulnerable in his or her expression too? Can you see one thing in the shape of a person's mouth and the opposite in his or her eyes? To do so is to practise the habit of objective observation so that it can become a stronger reflex in you.

Building a picture of the child

Steiner practitioners combat this natural tendency to slip into the subjective by always beginning with a physical description of the child. They begin by describing what the child looks like, the proportions of different parts of the body, the proportions of the features on the face, the child's colouring and the texture of the skin and hair. They then go on to describe how the child moves. This could be done verbally, including finding an image such as a mouse or a cat, for example, or a practitioner might even try to 'put on the child's shoes' and walk like him. Movement also includes how the face moves and how the arms and hands move when children expresses themselves. Next, what does the child sound like? Volume, pitch, articulation, modulation, disturbances, breathiness and typical expressions can all be mentioned. The practitioner might try to imitate their speech. By beginning with this kind of description of what the sense organs tell about the child, there is more chance of objectivity than talking about the child in an unstructured way.

Practitioners then use other aspects to build up a real living picture of the children. How do they eat? Like a bird or a dog? What are their likes and dislikes? Moving on to evidence of personality traits observed, how do they think? Is this child a clear thinker with a grasp of memory, practical intelligence and an ability to learn things quickly? Are they able to tell a coherent story? How do they deal with their emotions and how do they interact socially? The practitioner must take great care to find the words and remain objective when answering these kinds of questions. How do the children express their feelings? Are there examples of their perseverance, concentration and ability to assert themselves? How do they respond to themselves, the world and others? By working with questions such as these, especially in the company of a group of colleagues who all know the children, practitioners have the opportunity to really 'get inside their skin' and will certainly come to a deeper understanding of the nature of their children. A typical structure for a child observation is given in Appendix IV.

A recent research document on the topic of observation and assessment in Steiner kindergartens gives the following summary:

> Steiner educators are skilled and subtle observers of their children. They become familiar with the predictable signs and stages of development on the child's journey towards readiness for formal teaching, which replaces unconscious imitation and exploration as the principal mode of learning during the seventh year. They observe children closely, trying to understand them at every moment, alert for change but never judging. Drawing on their knowledge of the developmental process, the educators watch, listen and use their intuition to determine their particular response to the changing needs of the individual child. 'What can I do to help you?' is the unspoken question they carry: it refers not to the reaching of attainment targets but to the child's all round well-being, sense of self and individual interests and intentions.
>
> (Drummond and Jenkinson 2009: 46)

Practitioners believe that it is ideal to have the opportunity to watch the children when they are engaged in freely chosen play. Watching children at play shows what they look like when they are engaged in a situation rather than looking at an adult who is looking at them. Working quietly nearby, an adult can observe their speech and movements and also see what enthuses them, what they need to play out. If they are playing in a group, their social skills can be seen in action. It is also valuable to look at children's drawings and paintings and 'see' them in those too.

The concern is to build up a picture that is true to the child, but it is inevitably someone's picture, coloured by that person. It will be found that there is more of an emphasis on certain aspects than on others. There may be a lot to say about this child's speech, for example, or the social behaviour of another. One child's drawings might be particularly expressive of important things about him or her.

The practice of child study

Child study is an attempt to take the picture-building exercise to a deeper level and normally involves working with colleagues. Children's parents may also be asked to contribute. A child study is a process that takes place over time. First, the child to be studied is chosen. Unless the group of children is very small, it is not possible to do a child study for every child. However, the act of regularly following this process is one that benefits all the children. Through it the adults practise and extend their capacities to understand all children better. Sometimes a child is exhibiting difficulties in the group and presents challenges that the adults have not yet found satisfactory ways to meet. Or a child might be going through an unusual situation in his or her family life that suggests a need to penetrate more deeply. If the practitioner is experienced in undertaking child studies, then these are the kinds of children who may be chosen, but when the process is not firmly embedded in the pedagogical practice of the setting then individuals who present fewer challenges might be chosen at first. There is also value in choosing a child who is easily overlooked, the quiet one who apparently asks little of the practitioner, in order to bring to that child a focus that they do not usually receive.

Initial picture building

Once the child for the child study has been named, then all the adults in the setting will endeavour to observe that child for a few days. One person, usually the practitioner but perhaps an assistant or a student working in the setting regularly, then makes the initial presentation, beginning with the physical description, trying to remain objective and building up a word picture of the child. The adult's aim is to make it possible for everyone listening to hold in the mind's eye the same picture of the child as they do. This might take half an hour or more, and the other adults taking part will also have the opportunity to contribute their own additions or tweaks to the picture that is being presented. It may happen that someone even has a view of the child that is quite the opposite of the one that the practitioner is presenting. This would be interesting to note but one does not necessarily have to choose between the two opposite views. This reminds us that, despite our efforts to bring objectivity to our observations and our choice of words, different people may see a child, or an adult, from quite different perspectives.

If the parents have been involved in the child study, which is not always possible for practical reasons, it is often noteworthy how they see the child's interests and enthusiasm and characteristic behaviours. Is their view very different from the one that has been formed in the setting? Involving the child's parents in the study certainly will add an extra dimension to the discussion but some might feel that a more professional atmosphere is needed, and one alternative to full involvement is that an overview of the whole child study might be shared and reviewed with the parents by the practitioner after the event.

Developing the biography

There are some imaginative but revealing questions that might be asked at this point. For example, if this child were a landscape, what kind of landscape would he or she be: a flowery meadow, a stormy sea or a windswept mountain peak? If this child were a character in a fairy tale, which one would she be? One of the characteristics of fairy-tale characters is that they are archetypes, often not even given names in the oldest versions of these traditional tales (see Chapter 7). It can often be helpful to consider whether in this child, male or female, can be seen the attributes of the proud princess, the young hero striving against seemingly impossible odds, the silent old man who helps in difficult situations or the servant girl working until her fingers bleed. Are there signs of the wild wolf, the evil witch or the tricky 'little man' in this child? And, of course, can the opposite be seen? The aim is not to come up with a definitive picture of the child, a photograph which once taken cannot be altered, but to create something that moves to show the child from different aspects, to give something of an all-round view. This is expressed by Patzlaff and Sassmannhausen as follows,

> The goal of these discussions is not to form any kind of judgement about a particular child, but rather to get nearer to the essence of the child and gain a detailed understanding of his or her developmental situation, in consideration of all the anthropological, medical, and social conditions that are present, in order to arrive at providing appropriate help.
>
> (Patzlaff and Sassmannhausen 2007: 141)

Also to be considered is the child's biography which has helped to form them. Are they an only child, the eldest in the family, the middle one or the youngest, and how close in age are the siblings? What is the home life like and how has it changed during the child's life? Have there been any serious illnesses or accidents, and how did the child cope with these? Does this child live in a country setting or an urban one? Is it a peaceful house or a chaotic one? Does this child have a long journey to the setting by car, or by public transport, or does the child walk to school? There are many details that might add to the richness of understanding, but the process is to keep these biographical points until after the full description of what the adults have observed about the child has been given and has had time to sink in, so biographies may even be given a week after the initial picture-building. The endeavour is to avoid the danger of 'typecasting' the child with outside knowledge – 'of course, she likes to dominate the play, she is the eldest of three', for example. It will almost certainly be the case that the practitioner is well aware of the child's background through the initial conversation with the parents before the child joined the setting and regular subsequent exchanges. However, this information may not be available to all the adults undertaking the study and not to have it can often add to the freshness of their observations and thus help the practitioner to see the child with new eyes.

Some people choose to close the child study at this point. By the attention that the participating adults have paid to the child and the work that they have done together, a broader deeper picture has been built and, unconsciously, the child has felt that warmth of the interest. This process may already have changed the adults' responses to the child. If the child is a challenging one, this process will have given everyone more understanding of the child's experiencing, and a perplexing difficulty may be transformed into an opportunity to support the child in a new way. The adults might return to this child study one or even three weeks later and share any experiences of changes in the child that have happened since the initial child study.

Developing the child study

Where there is an experienced group of colleagues and a long practice of conducting child studies, it is possible that further steps can be followed. Taking things further requires courage as well as experience, and there could be dangers. It is important to avoid labelling children, and the aim is not to find a neat pigeonhole in which the child will fit. It is a priority to give the child room to change. But it is possible to take the child study further, drawing some conclusions about the child from the discussions that take place during the study and deciding on a programme of action. The child-study process is a deep one, and it is to be hoped that the discussion will go beyond the regular pattern of plan, do, evaluate and plan again. The child study is described by Steiner practitioners as a spiritual deed undertaken by the adults for the child, and each session of the study will normally begin and end with a specially selected verse or short meditation to bring to mind the child and mark that this is a special time for him or her. There are many verses, prayers and meditations which Rudolf Steiner gave to be used by teachers. The Steiner practitioner therefore considers that when a child study is conducted the wish of the adults to understand the child better and their work together for this aim, calls on the help of spiritual powers.

It must be acknowledged that the practitioner can't make a child different. All that can be done is to work on adults' attitudes and responses to the child in order to support and strengthen their own healthy inclinations to change. So if we wish to change the child, we must endeavour to change ourselves. A point is reached at which Steiner pedagogy says that it is the self-development of the adult that is significant.

It is the inner striving of the adult that is crucial in the quality of his or her work with young children. This is not a substitute for knowledge of child development and appropriate early-childhood methodology, but it is vital nevertheless that the practitioner is always active in this area, both in initial training and as continuous professional development.

The use of assessment

According to Mary Jane Drummond, 'Effective assessment is a process in which our understanding of children learning, acquired through observation and reflection, can be used to evaluate and enrich the curriculum we offer' (1993: 13). This definition of assessment fits well with the process of objective observation and child study described previously. To whatever level this is taken, it is based on the practitioner's underlying question, 'What do I notice going on?' This kind of assessment is common practice in all Steiner Waldorf early-childhood settings. Each child will have a file in which records are kept of enrolment documents, initial and subsequent conversations with parents and other things that help to build a picture of the child's journey through the setting or school. Practitioners keep individual child record sheets where noticeable details about the child can be kept alongside information that may come from parents and carers. It is interesting and telling to note how for some children this is a small document and for others there might be extensive daily entries at times. There will be examples, including photographs, of the child's art work and play and contributions from the lead practitioner and from assistants. The aim is to keep a rich record of the child's history in the setting while remembering that it is a history and tomorrow may be different!

Summative assessment

Summative assessment has been accepted more slowly into Steiner practice. There has been a natural reluctance to take on a 'tick box' profile that seems to be so at odds with our ways of working and to look at children in terms of 'outcomes'. That the EYFS (that is the Early Years Foundation Stage, a regulatory framework applied to all English early-years education and care settings outside the home) regulations have obliged practitioners to complete such a tick-box form for all children rising school age has added to this reluctance, when practitioners have struggled to see value in a profile based on learning goals that do not fit the Steiner Waldorf early-childhood curriculum. However, there is now an understanding that summative assessment has a place in the Steiner kindergarten as long as formative assessment practices, such as work with objective observations and child studies, are kept strong. A variety of Steiner Waldorf early-childhood assessment documents are being trialled, and work has been done internationally to produce a summative assessment document more in keeping with the activities of a Steiner kindergarten, but as yet this Steiner Waldorf profile is a working document that is still being developed.

The way in which the practice of Steiner settings complies with EYFS requirements in fully explained in the booklet *Guide to the Early Years Foundation Stage in Steiner Waldorf Early Childhood Settings*, a document specifically prepared to explain our practice in the vocabulary of the EYFS (SWSF 2009). This will change depending on the new EYFS Framework criteria.

Children requiring additional support

The Steiner Waldorf early-childhood setting is an enabling environment, as discussed in Chapter 4. It is to be hoped that the environment and activities of such a setting will enable a group of children to flourish and develop happily and healthily together. Practitioners will plan and prepare, working with yearly, weekly and daily rhythms, a programme that will meet the children's needs. Through observations and reflection, plans will be adapted and refined day to day. But the responsible practitioner has to acknowledge that there are sometimes individuals whose needs ask more than the setting and its normal way of running can provide. It is the combination of summative and formative assessments that will be most helpful here, providing a picture that can be discussed with parents and shared with professionals such as school doctors, therapists and special educational needs specialists both within the school and in the wider community. It is absolutely necessary that records be made and kept that will be helpful in such situations, and Steiner practitioners fully acknowledge this responsibility.

Child study and all that is involved in it calls on adult creativity as well as professionalism and self-development. The ability to respond to a child in the moment comes from deep understanding based on observation, but it also calls on the adult to use imagination, intuition and inspiration. Again it is the willingness of the adult to engage with the big questions that supports this kind of development. 'How can I understand my life and those of others, how can I become a better person, how can I help to make the world a better place?' These are questions that Steiner pedagogy would expect the children in Steiner settings to be tackling, albeit unconsciously. The Steiner practitioner believes that, if we are worthy to be carers and educators, we must be ready to work with questions like this ourselves and thus endeavour to become the flexible and responsible people that young children need.

Key points

1. Understanding children is based on knowledge of child development and on observations of children.
2. The Steiner practitioner tries to hone skills of objective observation and uses observation exercises to practise this.
3. This is aided by beginning an observation of a child by focusing on a description of the physical aspect of the child and using a thorough schema for this.
4. Watching the child engaged in self-initiated play is important.
5. In Steiner pedagogy, child study, usually done with colleagues, is an endeavour to deepen this observation process.
6. In a child study, one person will present the study, trying to build up a rich picture of the child, and colleagues, and sometimes parents, also have the opportunity to contribute.
7. The child's biography is presented at the end in order not to colour the picture from the beginning.
8. The aim is to reach the essence of the child and from that come to ideas of what might best help them.
9. Once again, the practitioner's commitment to self-development is significant.
10. The Steiner practitioner undertakes both formative and summative assessment and record keeping, in line with current regulations and in ways that compliment Steiner pedagogy.

Reflections

Child observation

- Can you think of some examples of objective and subjective ways of describing a child?
- Using the schema given in Appendix IV, describe child you know well and consider that value of this process. Has it given you a deeper understanding of the child?

■ Discuss your picture with colleagues who also know the child and notice where observations appear to clash.

Deepening child observation

■ Experiment with and discuss some of the deeper child study questions such as 'what kind of landscape would this child be?'
■ Consider that dangers both of hanging too much on your knowledge of a child's biography and of pigeonholing a child with a diagnosis.

Child assessment

■ Discuss the value of both formative and summative assessment.
■ What kind of record-keeping do you regard as most helpful?
■ What kind of record-keeping enables you to assess a child's additional needs?
■ Can you imagine at what points a Steiner Waldorf child profile might differ from the EYFS profile?

References

Drummond, M. J. (1993) *Assessing Children's Learning*, Abingdon: David Fulton.

Drummond, M. J. and Jenkinson, S. (2009) *Meeting the Child: Approaches to Observation and Assessment in Steiner Kindergartens*, Plymouth: University of Plymouth.

Patzlaff, R. and Sassmannshausen, W. (eds.) (2007) *Developmental Signatures: Core Values and Practices in Waldorf Education for Children 3–9*. New York: AWSNA.

Steiner, R. (2008) *Educating Children Today*, London: Rudolf Steiner Press.

SWSF (2009) *Guide to the Early Years Foundation Stage in Steiner Waldorf Early Childhood Settings*, Forest Row: SWSF Publications.

10 Working at partnerships to support the child

Introduction

In this chapter we will be looking at how parents, educators, support staff and others can work together to support the children in our care. Working with parents is of particular importance, and we will see how through study, research, education and observation both the family and the children can be supported and included in the life of the kindergarten and beyond.

The importance of personal relationships

We are aware, as parents and educators, of the importance of attachment for the young child. There is much research to underpin our knowledge of how personal relationships affect the development of the young child either in giving nourishment and building up physical organs or in causing long-term damage both physically and emotionally. This is well documented by researchers such as Bowlby (1979) and Gerhardt (2004).

It is accepted that the quality of the environment, whether at home or in childcare, is important if not essential for healthy all-round development. The physical, emotional and verbal environment and the interaction with adults contribute to later outcomes and may affect the child's life chances, educational possibilities and intellectual and social development as an adult. Nurturing support is a stronger predictor of children's all-round achievement than any material circumstances of their upbringing. It is the quality and content that matters, not the education and income of the parents (Allan 2010).

Working with parents

Parents are children's primary attachment figures, even if they spend much of the time in childcare. It is vital that the Steiner practitioner can share with the parents the picture they have of the child as a special individual, a child bearing gifts. Trusting, open cooperation with the parents is essential as educators need to share practice and pedagogy as well as the natural rhythms and good habits that govern the Steiner approach to childcare.

Parental participation in the life of the kindergarten and sharing the support and nurturing of the child together are of the greatest importance for the child's development. Depending on the possibilities or restrictions placed on the parents by their employment they may have much or little time to be involved in the life of the kindergarten or to interact with the practitioner, or even to spend with their child. All of this needs to be kept in mind when planning settling in, supporting transitions, giving feedback, participating in festivals and celebrations, parents' evenings and home visits. It is also possible that the parent would rather be spending their time with their child and already feels guilt about putting them in childcare – therefore the practitioner has to be careful not to add to this burden by having unreasonable expectations of the parent.

Initial meeting and child profile

In the majority of Steiner settings, parents either bring their child into the kindergarten via the school's parent and child group or apply directly to the kindergarten without any previous experience or understanding of Steiner early-childhood care and education. The initial meeting between the parents, and including the child, is therefore an important one. Sometimes the meeting takes place after the parents have attended an open day or have had an informal visit to the setting. (This visit can also take place after the meeting in the term before the child is due to attend the kindergarten.) The initial meeting however, is for the parents and practitioner to get to know and to find out about each other and for the parent to share their picture of the child's developmental (from birth), including details of the child's physical and emotional development. This can be described as building a picture of the child, sometimes called a 'child profile'. It is an opportunity to share medical history, how the parents handle behaviour, family cultural and religious backgrounds and so on. The practitioner briefly explains the ethos of their kindergarten, its structure and philosophy, and answers any questions arising. Prior to the child joining, the settling in of the child is discussed. The picture of the rainbow bridge is one which is easy to share. The rainbow bridge is, in Steiner education, the one where the child comes from Heaven to their earthly home – the bridge to the world is through the kindergarten. The child stands on the centre of this bridge, the parents and home on one side, the setting at the other. Both need to hold it steady and keep the child at the centre. The final bridge that involves them both is the transition to school, where children leave not only the kindergarten but also their early childhood behind. Here the parents and practitioner stand together as the child makes his or her own way into the future.

Settling in

Establishing good contact and communication with the parents during this period is important, whether they stay for a few days to settle the child in or drop the child off. What is needed is to trust the process in place. Making time for a quick word at drop-off and collection times helps the parent to settle as much as the child. In fact, a confident, settled parent generally means a confident and more easily integrated child.

Parental involvement in the life and activities of the setting

There is an expectation from the setting that the active involvement of parents as partners in the education of their children takes place. That also means that parents are expected to attend the parent evenings, contribute to the ongoing formative assessments which the practitioners need and, as far as their individual circumstances allow, join in with activities such as festival preparation, redecorating the rooms, gardening work and the offering of structural, organisational and financial support. Parents are encouraged to share their own skills to contribute to the life and upkeep of the kindergarten. Many times in my own kindergarten I invited parents to help with repairs (the boys particularly loved it when their dads helped build or mend) or to share skills such as weaving, gardening or cooking.

Festivals and celebrations

There are many festivals and celebrations that involve parental or whole-family participation. Birthdays, for instance, play an important part in the life of the child and in the kindergarten yearly rhythm. The parents are asked to share the milestones of the child's development with the teacher, which are woven into a story to be told on the day. They are often invited to attend the session or the birthday celebration part. Siblings and grandparents can also attend in some settings. There are many festivals which are open to families, such as May Day, Advent Garden or Harvest. Puppet shows, fairs and other open days are generally public events where parents help, or attend with the whole family, bringing food, song, music and story or being there simply to enjoy themselves with their children and others. Building the 'kindergarten family' is important to everyone and particularly to the child.

Building the bridge between home and school

In Steiner education, it is considered important for the child's easy integration into the setting that the parents are able to adopt some of the educational practices and ethos into the home. The practitioner, and sometimes parents, organise study groups and workshops (craft and educational) for parents and other interested participants. Regular parent evenings are held where a picture is given of the kindergarten practice, play and of the children. They usually include a song or two and sometimes focus on a theme such as play, painting or festival. The parents join in, painting or baking as in the kindergarten, while explanations are given as to the pedagogical benefits for the children.

One-to-one meetings and home visits take place where the teacher can have more intimate exchanges with the parents about their child. Parents are also expected, where possible, to limit television or media exposure in the home, and they are provided with information about why this is considered best for the child. They are encouraged to develop a rhythmic home time, with few extracurricular activities for their children and to prepare food and eat together as a family where possible. They are encouraged to adopt the imaginative approach to equipment and especially to limit the toys at home, using natural materials if possible, dressing the children appropriately and making sure that the children have smooth transitions to bedtime, which includes a story and a song.

Steiner practitioners are aware that they ask a lot of the parents, and the parents are made aware that bringing the child to a Steiner Waldorf setting is about trust, self-development and, often, change. Parents tend to choose Steiner education specifically for their child, researching it before their visit. However, what they often say as soon as they enter the kinder-

Figure 10.1 Transition to school festival.

garten is how they feel themselves. The environment and mood impact on their feelings, their descriptions are full of adjectives, and, if asked to describe the experience, they talk about the gentle mood, the lovely colours, the warm and welcoming atmosphere, the lively play, the feeling of 'coming home', and they describe how they just 'know' in their bones, that this is the right place for their child. It does not mean that the transition will be easier, or that the questioning will be less; they believe just that, for the moment, this is the place where they and their child belong.

Working with colleagues

Because of statutory requirements in the UK, all kindergartens have two members of staff with the children at all times. In general this means an assistant for the kindergarten practitioner. The assistant has a very special role to play in the life of the kindergarten, and, in general, they are not the main focus for the children. (The 'key person' is the kindergarten teacher.) The assistant is there to support the practitioner, to carry out the day-to-day activities quietly and in a manner 'worthy of imitation' but not to lead the ring time, story or main activities unless requested. Frequently, assistants are training to become kindergarten teachers and, as such, have an opportunity to practise their study in a placement. They are given time to take a ring time or to do a puppet show and attend the parent meetings. They are seen as a partner and, in general, take part in all study, teachers meetings, celebrations and events. They may be given specific tasks, for instance, always to be aware of a specific child, or they could be in charge of preparing the snack, the table and so on. Assistants also participate in all the activities, joining in ring time or possibly sitting with a child who does not want to participate. They generally follow the lead of the practitioner throughout the session. It is always helpful if the assistant can participate fully in the child observations and study as well as in preparing the lesson plans, contributing to the daily review and the celebrations and festivals. There are occasions, usually if the setting runs for longer than four hours, when it is the assistant who carries the children through lunch and rest time, to give the teacher a break before the afternoon session commences.

Other colleagues also take part in the life of the kindergarten, such as the eurythmist, who comes in each week to do a movement session with the children or a foreign-language specialist who visits to do a French ring time, for example.

Parents and volunteers are always welcome, and many ex-Steiner school pupils from abroad, usually Europe, visit during their gap year, or as part of work experience. It is wonderful if these are young men who can opt to do this work instead of military service, and they are always a popular choice, as not only do they work well with the children but they are also handy around the kindergarten – building equipment or working in the garden or vegetable patch with the children.

Because the adults are aware that how they behave and even feel and think impacts directly on the children, they work hard at making sure that relationships are warm, loving and generous and that there are no personal issues carried into the kindergarten. There is generally no unnecessary conversation taking place while the children are present, and only what is important is spoken about. Looking only for the very best in each individual helps to make real collegial relationships work.

Working with doctors, therapists and early-years development specialists

It is important to recognise that individual children develop at different rates and in different ways; however, there are always those who fall outside normal parameters. In some cases, the ability or disability has already been recognised before the child attends the setting, but this is not always the case, as with children on the autistic spectrum, or those with attention deficit hyperactivity disorder or who have a tendency to dyslexia. Sometimes parents who have no specific contact with other children or for whom this is their first child do not recognise what might be outside the norm, and there are also cases where behavioural difficulties emerge later or once the child is with peers.

Help in these cases is always necessary, as although practitioners might be experienced or have had training with special needs, they are not therapists and should never diagnose. In these cases, detailed objective observations of the child and sometimes child studies take place and are discussed with the family who contribute to an individual education plan. If the situation needs further help, then specialists are called or the parents are asked to take the child to outside agencies for further opinions. There are many Steiner Waldorf therapists who are trained in different areas such as music, movement, speech, dyslexia, eurythmy and so on. There are also doctors who are anthroposophically trained general medical practitioners attached to Steiner schools, known as 'school doctors', who visit children in the classroom to observe and diagnose, if requested by the parent and practitioner. In general, the school doctor also helps with 'school readiness' transition issues, for instance if it is thought that the child is to be the youngest in the class and the kindergarten teacher thinks that he or she would benefit by having another year in kindergarten.

All practitioners are trained in special educational needs, safeguarding, first aid, etc., and have contact with local authorities who they can also call on for help and advice. There are also occasions when the help of an individual support assistant is needed for a particular child in the kindergarten. The practitioner works closely with them. Parents are consulted in every area where their child is concerned, and all kindergartens are fully inclusive.

Key points

1. Steiner practitioners work with parents to form a joint picture of the child and to learn as much as they can about the child and family's history.
2. The Steiner Waldorf approach includes the concept of the key person and focuses on building relationships with the child.
3. The Steiner practitioner will usually visit the parents and child in their home.
4. The Steiner practitioner will work closely with the parents to support the child's transition to the setting, including settling in with the parents' support.
5. Parents will be provided with information on the child's development and care, both verbal and written.
6. Special events, such as birthdays, are often shared with parents in the setting.
7. The Steiner setting will provide festivals, workshops and information for parents on the ethos and practice of Steiner education.
8. There will be opportunities for families and friends to share their enthusiasm and skills in the kindergarten setting.
9. The practitioner will make contact with 'outside' services to support the child in areas of special need.
10. There are also Steiner-trained specialists to diagnose, offer advice or support the child.

Reflections

Supporting transitions

- How do you provide for a smooth transition into the setting for child and family?
- Do you have a 'key person' system to support secure attachments?
- How do you provide for parents in the life of the setting?
- What is in place to support the child's transition from your setting to school?

Festivals and celebrations

- How do you provide for parents in celebrating religious or cultural festivals without being tokenistic?
- How do you involve parents in celebrating their child's birthday?

Home–school integration

- In what form do you provide parents with your vision and ethos, and in which way could you develop a shared picture of their child?
- Do you see the value of home visits and what would you, the child or the family expect to gain from this?
- What aspects of your practice would you like your parents to adopt in order to support their child?

Working with colleagues

- Who do you share the care of the children with in the setting, and how is this organised?
- How do you enable positive relationships with colleagues?
- How are leadership roles structured, and does this allow for difference?
- Which outside specialists do you feel would help support you and the children in your care?

References

Bowlby, J. (1979) *The Making and Breaking of Affectional Bonds*, London: Routledge.

Gerhardt, S. (2004) *Why Love Matters*, London: Routledge.

Graham Allan Review into Early Intervention 2010. www.dwp.gov.uk.

11 Current issues

Introduction

Steiner early-childhood education and care in the UK is part of a fast-growing worldwide movement. It incorporates everything from parenting, childcare and day care to the training of educators. In this chapter we will highlight some areas of current interest and those which are being developed according to the principles and ethos of Steiner Waldorf education and care. Some of what follows has been further developed in previous chapters.

Birth to three

There has been a worldwide interest in expanding and deepening Steiner Waldorf knowledge and pedagogical approach to the very young child (before the age of three). An international group has been studying this in conferences and groups, and from it comes a better understanding not only about the stages of development but also about how to enable children to integrate with their physical body, with social relationships and with the wider world. The educators are also discussing what new training is needed to build the qualities and competencies to be good role models for this age group. Particularly important is how to work with the parents in partnership. Much of this is explained in *The Child from Birth to Three in Waldorf Education and Child Care* (Patzlaff et al. 2011), including the development and structure of the physical body and the effect of early formal education on later learning.

It is this structuring of the physical organisation, especially of motor and sensory functions, that creates a firm foundation for the healthy activity of soul and spirit in later life. The outward-directed development prepares the stage that is inward-directed. Children have to be able to stand before they can understand the world; they have to be able to touch and grasp things physically before they can grasp them mentally; they must smell and taste things, touch and feel them with their hands in order to experience the world as tangible, comprehensible and transparent. What appears later as the capacity of thinking is not built up by intellectual understanding but by 'hands-on' activities in early childhood, because these activities have a structuring effect on the inner organs and the brain. The forces that build up and shape the body in early life are later transformed into powers of imagination, thinking and reflection.

If we allow children enough time to follow their natural inner urge for learning and doing and to experience this first fundamental developmental phase intensely, we can trust that the inward-directed metamorphosis from dependence on sensory impressions to the free use of mental activities will occur at the right time for each child. If parents and educators don't have this trust or knowledge, the maxim 'the earlier the better' will lead them to expect accomplishments from young children and infants that only schoolchildren or adolescents can manage. It is interesting that little research has as yet been conducted into whether very early formal teaching increases children's performance for years to come or whether it just creates a 'flash in the pan' effect. Waldorf education wants to achieve long-term success. Its maxim is, therefore, to allow children to proceed in their own time. The more time they have to develop fundamental capacities, the stronger they will be.

(p.12)

This approach, particularly to the first two years, has much in common with the Pikler method. Emmi Pikler (1902–84) was a Hungarian paediatrician who believed that children have an innate capacity to direct the unfolding of their motor capacities through self-initiated movement, if given the time and space to do so, and that infants should not be taught motor skills or pushed through the use of equipment such as bouncers and walkers but instead should be allowed gradually to come into the vertical positions of sitting, standing and walking entirely through their own efforts, unaided by adults. She felt that this self-initiated movement could only take place if the child was in a secure relationship with a primary adult, whether they were the parent, or a practitioner, commonly called 'caregiver' in Steiner practice. Adopting the Pikler approach in Steiner practice is a new and growing trend. In

America it is known as the Resources for Infant Educarers approach, which is based on the work of the early childhood educator Magda Gerber and Emmi Pikler.

There are also many baby groups where new parents and their babies come together with those who are more experienced in Steiner pedagogy to study parenting questions together. In some cases, this also includes a craft activity, food and drink and singing and provides new parents with a supportive group of friends and helpers.

Parent and child groups

Every Steiner school and kindergarten has a parent and child group attached; in fact, many of the schools' early beginnings were in such a group, where likeminded parents came together with their children to seek to understand the Steiner approach to parenting and childcare. Many groups are held in public halls, parents' houses or outdoors, or, if in a school, within a dedicated space and in a specially created and cared-for, peaceful, child-friendly environment within which parents with baby or toddlers (to around three years of age) can play and talk with each other.

The toys are similar to those offered in the kindergarten: carved wooden animals and toys, hand-sewn dolls and natural objects found on walks, e.g., conkers, pine cones and seashells (of suitable sizes of course). Lengths of dyed muslin are wrapped around screens to form cosy home corners and little dens.

The 'activity' provided is simple: baking together, painting or drawing, making toys for the group, or a simple seasonal craft activity such as making butterflies in the spring and conker webs in the autumn. Parent and child sit together, work together and learn together, handling the simplest of natural materials such as brightly coloured sheep's wool, cones and seeds, beeswax, muslin and silk. A simple activity can be done in silence, carrying a mood that suits the activity, or it could provide an opportunity to talk together, to share parenting issues and to make friends while being occupied in meaningful activity such as sewing the clothes the children use for dressing up.

In each session there is time for both play and craft activity which run alongside each other and transitions are supported by singing. There is always a little story time, often with puppets, and in many cases there is an opportunity for singing and movement in a circle, which includes familiar nursery rhymes and the seasonal songs of childhood. Everyone comes together at the table to share a snack of fresh food prepared together or brought each time by a different member of the group. A little song is sung to 'bless the meal' as a reminder of the importance of sharing with one another.

The morning finishes with time in the garden, meeting later in the goodbye circle, which is both an affirmation of time together as well as a reminder for everyone of future meetings.

Day care

In the UK there are a few Steiner full day-care centres for the child from around six months to seven years, running full days and fully inclusive and adapted to the needs of the children who attend, whether full-time, sessional or drop-in. Some take babies, some do not. Like everything else in Steiner early childhood, the intention is to involve the parents as much as possible in their child's education, care and environment. As in the kindergartens, there are opportunities to become involved by joining in events, festivals and celebrations. In many European countries where the provision of day care from babyhood onwards is long established, all-day Steiner Waldorf provision for the very young child is common.

Outdoor/woodland parent and child groups and kindergartens

There is a growing interest in outdoor groups, and a number of parent-and-child groups meet in open spaces and enjoy what nature has to offer (see Fig. 11.1). They follow a similar routine to the normal parent-and-child day and meet outdoors no matter what the weather has to offer, buggies and children permitting. The woodland kindergarten initiative is still in its infancy in the UK. There are no Steiner kindergartens that spend all of every session outside. Every kindergarten spends a part of every day outside as has already been discussed. Many settings do spend at least one session or day a week completely out of doors. This could be in the kindergarten's own grounds where these offer a suitably rich natural environment, in the local area (lanes, meadows and woods in a rural setting, streets and parks in the town) or perhaps in a nearby nature reserve.

Figure 11.1 Woodland shelter.

In some cases, a small shed, cabin or yurt provide shelter to rest and, if the weather is particularly bad, a place to eat if this is not taking place around an open fire. The weather is seen as part of the learning journey, and the whole experience helps to develop resilience and strength of purpose in the children as well as an appreciation of our natural world.

Steiner home childcare

Childminding and caring for young children, whether within the child's home or the carer's home, is a growing and flourishing initiative in the UK. Childminders enjoy the small groups, mixed ages and family activities which are so suitable for the home. There is specialist training available, and a network has formed, with discussion and study groups providing support. Networks of Steiner-inspired childminders can often be found where there is a Steiner Waldorf school or early-childhood setting.

Home schooling

There are many children following the Steiner approach who are educated at home. They have the benefit of subscribing to the many home-
school groups who give help and advice on the approach, not only to the
changing home lifestyle but also to the educational approach throughout
the school years. The families seek each other out to meet and share
experiences.

Wrap-around care

Many kindergartens cater for working parents and therefore offer wrap-
around care, where the child can come to the setting for breakfast and
stay after the session for lunch, a rest and an afternoon session which
consists mostly of outdoor play. The rhythm of the day is gentle, and
there is no repeat of the kindergarten morning but rather a gentle
progression to more relaxed play in the afternoon. Children can either
bring a healthy packed lunch, or an organic meal is cooked for them. In
the afternoon, as in the morning, they receive a welcome and nutritious
snack. There is always an opportunity and place for rest or even for sleep,
and children are encouraged to do so together.

Mixed ages in the kindergarten setting

The majority of kindergartens have at least three, and sometimes four
age groups within one setting. This contributes to the sense of family,
which is included in the so-called 'home like' environment of the kindergarten (see Chapters 4 and 5). The benefits of having this mixed-age
group are many and differ for each of the age groups. The younger
children are able to imitate or model the behaviour and impulses of the
older children. For instance, in the ring-time activity the younger children are 'carried' by the activity and enjoyment of the older ones. They
become aware of the many things that they will be able to do when they
are older and at first follow them unconsciously, then anticipate them,
such as lighting the candle before snack, which can only be done 'when
I'm big!' The older children can follow the journey they have had. They

have benefited from the repetition and routine of the kindergarten and they remember with joy the recurring festivals and events. They become confident in 'being able to do it by myself' and also being able to help those who are younger to deal with practical necessities such as zippers, buttons, washing up after lunch and helping the adults. They learn patience and compassion. The fact that the kindergarten enables this sort of socialisation to take place also helps develop capacities which will be lifelong.

The kindergarten teacher, however, will make sure that what is provided is developmentally appropriate for this mixed-age group and meets the needs of all the ages in different ways. Working with this 'wholeness' of the group as well as with each individual child is a challenge, particularly making sure that each child's learning journey and developmental progress takes place within the form provided by the rhythm of the kindergarten.

The older child (six to seven years old) and transition to school

Because new capacities come to life between five and seven years of age, the children's spontaneous activity becomes more organised and develops into purposeful activity. They have the ability to work on tasks independently, and instead of working out of unconscious imitation of the adult begin to observe carefully what is being modelled in front of them and to try and do it carefully and as well themselves. They unconsciously absorb the 'inner activity' of the teacher, and this helps them to develop a certain resilience, an active engagement with their own will (doing) activity, and now they also need to see that each task is completed and properly finished. This ability to follow a task through to its proper conclusion will stand them in great stead throughout their lives. It builds concentration and resilience.

In some kindergartens, children, in their last year, are given activities (pre-schools tasks) that help develop this resilience and will activity. They could make dolls, a hobby horse, a handwork or crayon bag for 'big school'. They could become the teacher's 'helper', taking on the task for a week or so of setting the table and serving the food, or making sure the plants are watered, or preparing the paints and paper. They could run errands, wash up, do the register or take care of a new child entering the group. All these could be considered activities suitable for this age, when the child is beginning to develop new capacities of empathy, responsibility and physical prowess.

The space and time provided for indoor and outdoor activity also provide an opportunity to explore their physical capabilities. They learn to skip, balance, climb and take risks, developing a sense of the limits and possibilities of their physical bodies. Formal teaching of writing, reading and number work are avoided, but the foundations for later formal learning are provided within the daily activities of the kindergarten. The development and use of language and terminology skills in combination and in application to concrete artistic craft and domestic activities build the foundations of pre-literate and pre-numerate abilities. 'School maturity' begins around the child's sixth birthday, which takes place in the kindergarten, and in Steiner schools children do not enter Class 1 of the school, or begin formal learning, until their seventh year. Within their last year of kindergarten, the teacher, together with the parent, builds up a detailed profile of the child, looking at their all-round capacities as well as their physical, educational and emotional development. In some schools, additional help is required to measure readiness for school and the school doctor or therapist is called on for advice.

In some of the small independent kindergartens, it is not always possible for children to progress to a Steiner school, and they therefore leave to continue in the local primary school. Parents try, where possible, to let them remain in the kindergarten until they are at least six, and may have to sign a home-school agreement to show that they are receiving full-time education. It does also depend on the registration with the primary school. If the primary school is oversubscribed and cannot offer a late place then the children will leave at four to join reception class. It is often the case that the families stay in touch and the children visit the kindergarten for festivals and events for many years afterwards.

Children progressing into Year 1 or 2, as mentioned previously, catch up very quickly with the literacy and numeracy, and, not only that: they are highly motivated and full of joy and enthusiasm for learning.

Technology

Children in the kindergarten are encouraged to develop skills and understanding in the use of technological tools, selected to enable the child to perceive, by observing and using, how the device works. Children can develop a feeling for mechanical and specialisation principles by making use of household and kitchen hand tools in play and purposeful group activities, using tools such as such as kitchen implements, woodwork tools, apple presses for making juice, cookers or outdoor ovens and levers and pulleys (see Fig 11.2). The devices that are used *reveal their working principles on the outside and in use*. This practice provides a very different learning experience to the use of closed-box technologies which require abstract reasoning to be understood and are appropriate learning tools for children at an older age.

Figure 11.2 Using a tool.

Steiner educators, and others, believe that if young children play with devices whose inner workings are hidden from their perception such as common electronic gadgetry, then their learning can focus too much on the pleasure that derives from the feeling of power that using specialised tools can provide. This feeling for power can then enter into and interfere with the child's natural healthy fantasy or physical understanding of how they interact with the world through a direct experience. The use of screen technology does not allow the child to integrate knowledge through their senses but actually reduces the sensory diversity and richness of human interaction. The voice coming through a loudspeaker, divorced from the screen image, is very different from the human inter-action of the storyteller's whole being, which is absorbed by all the senses of the child in a more integrated way. I remember once an ani-mated discussion amongst children about an elephant. An excited child exclaimed, 'I saw an elephant on TV, he was huge! He was *this* big' – and she held up her hands, measuring about 6 inches! The size of the elephant measuring 6 inches was a reality for this child, who could never comprehend the immensity of *elephantness*.

There is also a great deal of research such as that by Aric Sigman (2005) and Sue Palmer (2006) that shows that early introduction to media, par-ticularly to television, has serious consequences for children's develop-ment. You will never find any form of television, media or electronic gadgetry in a Steiner kindergarten, and parents are actively informed of the setting's views on its dangers for young children and are even discouraged from having it available in the home. However, today, most young children have experience of technological devices from their lives outside the kindergarten, and teachers answer questions helpfully and positively when children discuss something from their home life.

Too much too early . . . or laying the right foundations?

In Steiner education, it is, as you have seen from previous chapters, an established principle that children are not taught to read or write before rising seven. Formal learning, before this age, is achieved at a cost – often leading to anxiety, tension and low motivation to work at future stages. The foundations for formal learning, as previously explained, are laid in the first seven years, and children are well equipped, in fact are eager, motivated and confident, with good self-esteem and well-developed all-round abilities: they have concentration, pictorial memory, well-integrated small and large movements and coordination, can sit still and are extremely social.

The education seeks to nurture and protect the child's imaginative world, as this is seen as fundamental to healthy child development. Awakening the children's consciousness through direct teaching, questioning and reminding runs counter to this. Steiner educators wait for children to 'discover' and 'wake up', to 'become aware of' and 'begin to question' according to their individual development and readiness. Although the teachers may answer children's questions, these initially stem from the child's own experiences and self-initiated learning which is in effect the child's first research. Saying 'Well, I wonder,' when asked why the sun shines leaves the child free to pursue the answer themselves, and they do, coming up with an answer which is true for them: 'because it makes us happy' . . . well, doesn't it?

Praise and reproof are not necessary. In fact, they interfere with the child's freedom. By saying 'That's lovely', or 'Wasn't that nice?' or 'Well done!', the practitioner cuts into the unity between the child and his or her activity and becomes a 'judging' adult, undermining the child's confidence. There are other ways of affirming the child's action or honouring their behaviour or task. To do this the adults need to enter, through empathy, with the child's activity. For instance, if children bring a picture which they have drawn, we show affirmation by saying 'Thank you' with full concentration on that comment and on that moment. The practitioner observes the drawing and, if necessary, consciously affirms what has been observed: 'Your tree has apples on it!' The practitioner is not making judgements by looking at it from outside. 'I like the way you have drawn apples on your tree' is a personal statement. Awakening the child's self-consciousness is not encouraged. There is also no use of praise to motivate the child, and reliance on praise as a reward is discouraged. Rather, the teacher is grateful for the child's engagement, and being grateful for something requires a response. 'Thank you', with full consciousness, not an unconscious response, should be enough. Reproof should not be necessary in a direct way, but rather creative discipline is used: 'Hands are for good work' is used rather than 'It isn't nice to hit!' In this way the practitioner tries to support the child's behaviour in positive ways by emphasising how everyone can shine.

Mathematical concepts and language are integrated into the daily life of kindergarten and are thus embedded within a meaningful context. Likewise, everything the children experience within kindergarten fosters a love of language and the development of good vocabularies. In this way literacy is given the best possible foundation. As Steiner said in a lecture in 1923,

> Although it is highly necessary that each person should be fully awake in later life, the child must be allowed to remain as long as possible in the peaceful, dreamlike condition of pictorial imagination in which his early years of life are passed. For if we allow his organism to grow strong in this non-intellectual way, he will rightly develop in later life the intellectuality needed in the world today.
>
> (1943: 120)

Equal opportunities

Steiner educators have a view of the child rooted in the spiritual view of the human being and each individual as being unique and valuable and having a contribution to make. Each culture contributes to the human expression on earth and should contribute to building a society founded upon mutual respect, tolerance and cooperation between all human beings.

It appears, on visiting a kindergarten, that the education might have a Christian or Catholic basis, often confused because of some of the festivals such as Christmas, Candlemas, Michaelmas and St John's are often celebrated, or through the verses of thanks, reference to angels and because there might be a painting of Raphael's *Sistine Madonna and Child* (as explained in Chapter 4) hanging in the room. However, in most cases, what appears in practice is not necessarily the same as what is perceived. The festivals are celebrated in nature, and through the changes that naturally occur at certain times of the year. Easter, for instance, is a time when what is apparently dead or asleep comes to life: new buds on the plants, the emergence of the butterfly from the chrysalis and blossoms from branches – life resurrects itself each year anew. At Advent, in so many countries, there is a celebration of light in the darkness. Those normally celebrating Diwali, Hanukkah, Advent and many others delight in the Advent or Midwinter Spiral, where each child places his or her light in the world and together light up the 'garden' that makes their home.

Steiner education is an approach which can be adopted in any country. The Arab–Israeli kindergartens are working to bridge cultural and religious divides, as are those in Egypt, Iran and in South Africa, where the Waldorf schools were integrated despite opposition during the Apartheid regime, or in China, Nepal, Pakistan, India and so on. The educators all work with the image of a human family at peace with itself, respecting each of its members and recognising that each member of 'our' human family on earth has gifts to share, from which we can all benefit.

Because Steiner Waldorf is a world organisation, it is often the case that the kindergarten attracts families from many different cultures, who look on a later introduction to formal learning as the norm in their country. In the initial interviews, the cultural background, particular needs, religious belief and individual approach to family life is discussed with the parents and the ethos of the Steiner approach is explained. In some cases, parents or families are asked to share a special festival or celebration from their own culture with the setting (see Chapter 10).

Inclusion

Many families of children with additional needs seek out the Steiner early-childhood setting as an appropriate place for their child. The small class sizes, the family and homely atmosphere, the slow pace and the view of the child as an individual bringing gifts no matter what ability or disability all make this approach appealing to parents. Learning English as a second language is also welcomed, as the focus on clear good speech, imitation and example help the young child to 'absorb' language easily. Many kindergartens have access to support, either from their school doctor and special support department or have the possibility to access support from a nearby Steiner school or health centre.

The therapy or special support staff has generally had mainstream as well as Steiner curative and special-needs training. There are specially trained music, speech, eurythmy, Bothma gym and medical specialists who work therapeutically with the child in the Steiner Waldorf schools and settings. The school doctors are both fully qualified medical practitioners and have had anthroposophical medical training.

Kindergartens also have access to inclusion and special educational needs services through the local authority where necessary. There are occasions where a child with additional needs has one-to-one support from a learning support assistant, who accompanies that (and possibly other children) during their time in the setting. In some cases, providing support is not always possible due to lack of resources.

There are a number of specialist homes, schools and communities for children and young people in the Steiner education special schools sector. These apply an adapted Waldorf curriculum. For further information contact the Committee for Steiner Special Education or the Association of Camphill Communities via the SWSF website.

Eurythmy

Steiner was asked by a young woman to develop a form of movement based on anthroposophical thought. Together they created eurythmy, aiming to make visible in human gestures and movements the spiritual qualities of words and music: 'visible language and visible music'. It was developed first as a performance art and today encompasses education, therapy and social and business applications. Eurythmy is a form of movement that requires inward as well as outward mobility. The physical body becomes an instrument of movement, speech and music, making these things visible. It is an educational tool that helps pupils become aware of their physical bodies unconsciously, where the body becomes a reference point for what happens around them and where they become aware of their place in space and time. In early childhood, this happens unconsciously through imitating the activity and movements of the eurythmy teacher. Later in school it becomes conscious movement. It enables the creative forces that precede language and music to live in the movements. Awareness of the physical body is acquired by being active – by moving – and is the beginning of self-knowledge. For children this means that through movement, both conscious and unconscious, they become aware of their own functioning. Through movement and activity the children get to know their environment and become acquainted with the things around them as well as with their own movements. The inner movements one makes while thinking can be compared to the outer movements made while physically exploring something. In Steiner education these two processes are continually interconnected, not just because children like to move, and their motivation to attend school and learn is extended, but especially because learning processes backed up by movement obtain greater meaning.

Rudolf Steiner pointed out how the creative movements we use in language and music are related to the creative forces active in nature as well as to those that work in our physical organism. He said that when we do eurythmy with children we address their life forces which are the basis of their lifelong health.

In the kindergartens within a Steiner school, the eurythmy teacher comes to the kindergarten once a week and the session takes the place of the ring time, which is generally held mid-morning. Beginning with putting on special soft non-slip shoes and often accompanied by music played by the kindergarten teacher or assistant on simple instruments such as the glockenspiel or 'kinderharp' (a seven-stringed lyre), the children follow the teacher through imitated movements within a circle. This can take the form of songs woven together within a story and includes rhythm, rhyme and repetition. We have already explained in previous chapters how the Steiner practitioner brings ring time to the children every day. The weekly eurythmy ring time also includes movements and gesture specially chosen to suit the age range and is based on everyday activities, simple stories or fairy tales or what is happening in nature, but this will also reflect the relationship between the speech and the movements in a different way, which the eurythmist is especially trained to bring.

Curative eurythmy

Curative eurythmy may be used to help a child with learning difficulties or developmental problems. Specific exercises are given to individual children to help them with their physical and inner development. This type of eurythmy is prescribed by the anthroposophical school doctor and given by a specially trained curative eurythmist.

Key points

1. Birth to three work is a growing area of Steiner research and practice and includes reference to the Pikler and RIE approach as well as to specialist Waldorf practice.
2. Parent-and-child groups operate in or are attached to all Steiner settings and schools, and day care is a growing area that includes babies and young children.

3. Outdoor and woodland groups are very popular, and many settings go out for long walks or to the woods for whole days.

4. Steiner Waldorf home childcare (childminding) supports working parents for sessional or whole-day care across broad age ranges.

5. Waldorf home-school groups are centred throughout the UK and also worldwide, and are particularly popular in the USA.

6. Wrap-around care caters for working families and works with a gentle rhythm that never repeats the morning kindergarten session.

7. Children are not introduced to formal learning (reading and writing) until they start in Class 1 of the main school. Until that time they build the foundations for literacy and numeracy through the rich kindergarten curriculum.

8. Technology and electronic gadgetry is not part of the kindergarten and is discouraged in the home. Children learn through hands-on technological household tools such as woodwork equipment, pulleys and levers, through baking, sewing and other daily activities.

9. The kindergarten includes mixed ages in 'family' groupings, and the children can spend three or even four years in the same group until transition to school.

10. Children with additional needs are catered for and included in the life of the kindergarten, with additional support when required.

Reflections

The enlarged family group

■ How do you work with the wider family, including pregnant mums, babies, toddlers fathers, grandparents and carers?

■ Is it important to cater for these areas, and, if so, how would you do so?

■ What support would you put in place, and do you believe additional training is needed in these areas?

Outdoor walks and woodland kindergartens

■ Do you take the children out on walks or spend most of the day outdoors?

■ What do you think of going out as a group and not using free-flow garden or outside time?

- Would you consider spending time in the woods, forest or nature reserves as an important activity for children, particularly those suffering 'nature deficit disorder'?

Wrap-around care

- Have you thought of offering breakfast for children, and do they stay after the session?
- Do you think that a different form of session is needed in the afternoon?
- Is it healthier for children to stay in one setting rather than being taken to a variety of different activities after the session?

Mixed ages

- What do you think is a good range of ages to have in the setting?
- Would you have to plan different activities for different ages or would the children all do the same things according to their ability?

Technology and electronic gadgetry

- Do you think children should have access to all technology in the setting?
- How would you react if children become dependent on technology and would rather be on the computer or watching television than playing with others?
- Do you limit technological use?
- Do you consider that computers and television encourages independence or do they encourage solitary behaviour?

Extra lessons

- Have you offered extra lessons such as music and movement, massage, foreign languages or dance?
- Do you think this would benefit the child or offer more variety?

References

Palmer, S. (2006) *Toxic Childhood*, London: Orion.

Patzlaff, R. et al. (2011) *The Child from Birth to Three in Waldorf Education and Child Care*, Spring Valley, NY: WECAN.

Patzlaff, R. and Sassmannshausen, W. (eds.) (2007) *Developmental Signatures: Core Values and Practices in Waldorf Education for Children 3–9*. New York: AWSNA.

Sigman, A. (2005) *Remotely Controlled: How Television Is Damaging Our Lives and What We Can Do About It*, London: Vermillion.

Steiner, R. (1943) *Education and Modern Spiritual Life*, London: Anthroposophical Publishing Company.

SWSF (2009) *Guide to the Early Years Foundation Stage in Steiner Waldorf Early Childhood Settings*, Forest Row: SWSF Publications.

Appendix I
Steiner Waldorf education: Its challenges and possibilities worldwide

Introduction

There are many discussions taking place worldwide about the challenge of educating 'free human beings' in Steiner Waldorf education, within the context of our times and the various cultures in which the education finds itself growing. In this appendix we will look at the challenges facing Steiner Waldorf education today and the support offered to assist good practice, enabling environments, a variety of different types of settings, well-trained practitioners and happy parents.

Meeting the needs of the child: accountability

Steiner Waldorf education is not a product which can be purchased nor merely a method which can be adopted, and the values of the education often have difficulty when confronted by governmental standards of testing and conformity to the curricula of the various countries in which it is based. Accountability is an issue in many cases, and measuring student performance through standardised testing at the various ages and stages is always a concern when each child is seen as an individual in the Steiner view of the human being. The education of the child is a partnership between parents and teachers and is influenced by the society in which it is based. In Steiner Waldorf education it is a holistic learning that not only looks at the outcomes and influences on the individual but also on social responsibility in the group and for society in general. It is not only the meeting of the needs of the child, which is important, but it is also the meeting of the needs of the group as a community, a kindergarten family.

In many countries, Steiner Waldorf education is state-funded and fully supported, and in some cases it is also left free in the way it aligns with expected conformity to children's profiles, standards inspections and testing. In some cases, exemptions are granted in areas of the curriculum that cannot comply with statutory regulation, particularly in the UK, where in the early years exemptions are needed from the early introduction of formal education and technology. Inspections of Steiner schools and kindergartens are carried out by government inspectors, although many Steiner schools in the UK are inspected by an independent schools section service. The kindergartens, which are not integrated into Steiner Waldorf schools and are registered as early-years settings, are inspected by Ofsted, and for those children who have reached statutory school age (five years in the UK), it is necessary to be inspected twice.

Steiner Waldorf early-childhood education in the UK

In the UK, the education and care of children between three and five years is statutory. This is known as the early years foundation stage (EYFS). Prior to the introduction of the EYFS, Steiner kindergartens were independent, working alongside others such as Montessori, High Scope and other private and voluntary settings. They applied for funding when this became available and thus entered the discussion groups within the private, voluntary and independent sector. The SWSF appointed an early-childhood representative to keep abreast of political and statutory changes, to become involved with the inspectorates (including training them in the Steiner approach) and to integrate into the wider early-years movement in the UK. Local-authority advisers and other educators became aware of and interested in the Steiner approach, and all through the development of the foundation stage and then the EYFS frameworks, representatives from the Steiner movement found themselves engaged in consultation and discussions with many others in early-childhood education and care. When the EYFS was introduced in England, combining the welfare requirements with education and care into one statutory framework from birth to five (statutory school age), Steiner practitioners agreed that there was much in common with the ideals and the images portrayed in the principles (including many of the themes and commitments), such as the unique child, enabling environments and positive relationships. It was with the learning and development requirements that Steiner early-childhood practitioners and many parents who choose the education have had issues. The statutory nature of these has so far led to a bureaucratic process of having to apply for exemptions to those learning and development requirements which they could not meet because of difference of educational approach and ethos, such as those relating to reading, writing, letter and number formation and the requirement to have electronic gadgetry (computers and toys) in the room. During the review of the EYFS, the SWSF was consulted, and the new EYFS will hopefully allow for more inclusion, or further exemptions. At the time of writing this, it is too early to say what the outcome for Steiner early-childhood education will be.

There is also a growing interest from mainstream practitioners who have an interest in some aspects of the Steiner approach. Workshops and seminars as well as training sessions on the education approach are popular, as is storytelling, puppetry, and the Steiner approach to play. Many wish to and do visit Steiner settings, as seeing 'how it works' in practice is the best way to understand the approach.

Steiner Waldorf education worldwide

Almost 100 years after the start of the first Waldorf School in Stuttgart, Germany, Steiner Waldorf schools are flourishing worldwide, a few in the poorest and most afflicted regions in the world, the slums of Calcutta and São Paulo and the townships of South Africa, in Palestine and Israel and on the Indian reservations in the USA. There is even one providing education to the children of war-torn Sierre Leone. In Europe, where there are large state-funded schools, small initiatives are starting which have their roots in the countryside or in the inner-city slums. Many children are from single-parent families, or in care, and many settings integrate local and immigrant children along with those from the local Muslim Turkish community together with Catholic Gypsy Travellers. In Israel, a combined Arab–Israeli kindergarten is flourishing, with Palestinian Muslims and Israeli Jews integrating together as families supporting their children in the joint community of the kindergarten. In America, there are independent schools, as well as 'charter' (funded) functioning in freedom.

There is a wish to offer the Steiner Waldorf free and creative universal education to whomsoever would choose it, regardless of religion, income, culture or government restrictions. Pluralism is now written into

European law, along with the rights for parents to choose the education for their child, and there is a hope that these principles will one day enable Steiner Waldorf free education to be offered worldwide. At present there are over 1,000 Steiner schools and over 2,000 independent kindergartens plus many new initiatives worldwide in over sixty-one countries. In the UK, there are many registered Steiner Waldorf schools and kindergartens. For a full list, see the SWSF website (http://www.steinerwaldorf.org).

The European Council of Waldorf Education

The European Council for Steiner Waldorf Education (ECSWE; see http://www.ecswe.org) comprises twenty-six national Waldorf associations, representing over 650 schools in Europe. Their aims are to facilitate the exchange of information and experiences in order to develop educational practices, to create and coordinate a common policy on a European level and to engage in dialogue with fellow educationalists, academics, politicians and education policy-makers.

Teacher education and other training

To work in the UK, the training to become a Steiner Waldorf practitioner has to include statutory workforce requirements. It is immensely practical and has as much to do with the transformation and development of the individual who is undertaking it as with the pedagogical content. Practice-based research is essential, as is the anthroposophical understanding of the developing human being. Practice and immersion in the arts, storytelling, puppetry, painting, drawing, woodwork, sewing, felting, eurythmy and so on are the basis for this transformative self-development as well as for developing new and existing skills. Students seeking to train have varied life experiences and come seeking answers to questions they have about childhood today, education or the human being. There are Steiner Waldorf training opportunities in parenting, parent-and-child work, day care, childminding, early childhood, school class teaching or specialist subjects such as speech, art and various therapies. Further information on training is available on the SWSF website.

The education is part of a worldwide movement, and although many countries have their own statutory requirements, the training also needs to follow the guidelines for Steiner Waldorf educators as agreed by the International Association for Steiner Waldorf Education (IASWECE). These Steiner Waldorf qualifications are internationally transferable.

The SWSF and the Steiner Waldorf Early Years Group (SWEYG)

The SWSF represents Steiner Waldorf education in the UK and Ireland. It is a registered charity that carries responsibility for advice, curriculum research, quality care and accreditation. Its remit covers support for legal and administrative matters, conferences, teacher training, contact with national media, international information, publishing and translating resource material, books and articles and a newsletter. The website includes links to other Steiner Waldorf organisations and schools within the UK and abroad as well as to initiatives, kindergartens and schools registered with them in the UK. The SWSF also carries the trademark for Rudolf Steiner and Waldorf education, and any schools, kindergartens or establishments using those names have to undertake an accreditation process through the SWSF. There are many initiatives currently working with the Steiner approach, and they receive support from trained advisers who are part of the SWSF advisory service.

The Steiner Waldorf Early Years Group (SWEYG) is a group who meet each term and consists of trainers, advisers and elected regional representatives. They organise local workshops and conferences so that practitioners can meet and study together. National conferences are also offered on a regular basis to provide continued professional development.

The advisory service, accreditation and registration

Quality childhood settings practise continuous self- and peer assessment, are visited by the SWSF early-childhood advisers, provide a sympathetic ear and eye and give advice and, hopefully, inspiration. They also provide help and support on the journey through accreditation from initiative to fully recognised Steiner early-years setting or centre and, in some cases, eventually to a becoming a full school.

Research

There are many research projects with interest in a variety of aspects of the education. At present, an in-depth research into the learning of English as a 'foreign' language, without resort to individual tutoring, is of great interest. Also, the introduction of two extra languages from the first school class is being researched. Creativity, drawing, conflict resolution, leadership and management, imitation, allergies, observation and assessment (meeting the child in Steiner Kindergartens), etc., are all topics of current academic research in Steiner Waldorf settings and schools.

There are a number of websites where information on research can be found, such as those of the Waldorf Research Educators Network (http://www.ecswe.org/wren/index.html) and the Research Institute for Waldorf Education (http://www.waldorfresearchinstitute.org).

The International Association for Steiner Waldorf Early Childhood Education (IASWECE)

Representatives of the various country associations who are members of IASWECE work together to deepen and renew the work with the young child out of the cultural impulse of Rudolf Steiner and the worldwide Steiner Waldorf movement. The aims of IASWECE include:

- fostering training and continuing development opportunities for care-givers, kindergarten teachers and educators;
- undertaking and supporting collaborative research on contemporary questions regarding the care and education of the young child;
- collaborating with parents, other educators and wider society about the needs of the young child;
- providing resources, information and publications;
- offering support – human, educational and financial – for new projects seeking to foster Waldorf early-childhood education throughout the world, particularly in developing countries.

(See www.iaswece.com)

Irish Steiner Kindergarten Association (ISKA)

ISKA provides support for members in the Republic of Ireland as well as responding to the increasing level of interest in Steiner Waldorf early-childhood education more generally in Ireland. The association has established a programme of workshops on aspects of Steiner Waldorf education for childcare practitioners and it runs a three-year part-time training programme. ISKA provides general advice, support and information on ISKA services, talks, workshops, annual conference and a newsletter as well as pedagogical and quality assurance support and mentoring for kindergartens and members in Ireland.
(See www.steinerireland.org)

The Alliance for Childhood

The Alliance for Childhood serves as a network that facilitates reflection and action by people with concerns about the care and education of children. It is not a conventional organisation but an expression of a willingness to work together for the betterment of the experience of childhood. It exists in the shared work and spirit of cooperation whereby all partners can find mutual support. It is a collaborative approach that is created by commitment and by the activity itself.

The Alliance works internationally, nationally and locally by:

■ exchanging information, research and experience, thereby building up a shared picture to allow individual initiative;
■ collating regular reports from around the world;
■ disseminating information through conferences, publications, the media and the Alliance website;
■ promoting research and identifying conditions for healthy child development;
■ encouraging joint activities between a range of community-based organisations involving children and adults;
■ working with government agencies to influence change in laws and policies.

You can find a list of the Alliance Worldwide partners on the website, http://www.allianceforchildhood.org.uk

The Association of Camphill Communities

Camphill communities are residential 'life-sharing' communities and schools for adults and children with learning disabilities, mental-health problems and other special needs, which provide services and support for work, learning and daily activity, where everyone lives, learns and works together with others of all abilities in an atmosphere of mutual care and respect. It includes independent residential and day schools, specialist colleges of further education and adult communities where each individual's abilities and qualities are recognised and nurtured as the foundation for a fulfilling life. In addition to caring for each other, those who make their lives at our Camphill centres care for the land and the environment around them by following organic and biodynamic principles in their gardens and on their farms.

All are caring, life-sharing communities, where the contribution made to community life by each person is valued. Everyone is appreciated for who they are, for their unique personality and for the special qualities they bring to community life.

Camphill community life is based on the teaching of Rudolf Steiner and is an initiative for social change inspired by anthroposophy. There are more than 120 Camphill communities in over twenty-one countries in Europe, North America, southern Africa and Asia where those with special needs are offered the support they need to develop their potential.

Appendix II

Typical equipment and activities in a Steiner Waldorf early-childhood setting

Typical equipment

- wooden play stands/clothes horses;
- wooden stools, crates, planks and boxes;
- plain-coloured cotton cloth and muslin veils, large and small;
- baskets of pine cones, pebbles, large and small logs, shells;
- woollen cords;
- small pieces of silk;
- simple cloth dolls and puppets;
- simple wooden and knitted animals.

Seasonal activities

Spring

- gardening and sowing seeds;
- blowing and painting eggs;
- making fleece chicks;
- making tissue-paper butterflies;
- making May crowns.

Summer

- watering and weeding the garden;
- washing, carding and dyeing fleece;

- modelling with beeswax;
- making paper birds and alder cone and wool bees;
- making popcorn on the fire;
- laundry.

Autumn

- harvesting and drying herbs;
- harvesting vegetables and fruit;
- jam-making;
- raking leaves;
- making leaf garlands;
- making simple kites;
- planting bulbs.

Winter

- making lanterns;
- making candles;
- collecting and sawing wood;
- making bonfires;
- feeding the birds;
- making evergreen wreaths;

All-year-round activities

- preparing our food (baking, scrubbing, peeling and chopping, milling, setting the table and washing up, etc.);
- cleaning and caring for our indoor and outdoor spaces (sweeping, dusting, polishing, washing, raking, etc.);
- making and repairing toys (sewing, woodwork, working with fleece and yarn);
- preparing for and celebrating festivals, including birthdays.

Appendix III

An example of a seasonal ring time for October

Song

Let us form a ring and we shall dance and sing,
Ringa-ringa-reia, ringa-ringa-reia.
Now we can all turn around, watch the birds fly up and down,
Kickeri-kickeri-kee!

Come follow me . . .

Song and dance

Our boots are made of leather, our stockings are made of silk,
Our pinafores are calico, as white as any milk.
Here we go, around, around, around,
Around, around, around.
Here we go, around, around, around,
Until we reach the ground.

In the morning, the farmer gives a big stretch – ah.
And he says . . .

Poem with actions

Good morning dear earth,
Good morning dear sun,
Good morning dear stones.
And the flowers, every one,
Good morning dear animals,
And the birds in the tree,
Good morning to you,
And good morning to me.

After he has eaten a lovely bowl of porridge – mm,
He puts on his boots, one for stumper and one for jumper,

And he calls all the children to help him start work . . .
He fetches his old leather bag down from its peg in the barn,
And he goes to the seed bin and opens it to fill the bag with wheat.
Scoop and pour, scoop and pour, scoop and pour.
Shut the lid to keep out the mice and we are ready to go to the field . . .

Song

On a Monday morning, a sunny Monday morning,
We sowed our field, Father and I,
We sowed in when the sun was high,
We sowed our field, Father and I,
Sowed it when the sun was high.

When the field was all sown, there was a little handful of grain left in the bottom
of the bag, so we tipped it out under a bramble bush on the way home.

After the farmer had gone home, the seagulls came singing and looking for
food . . .

Song

Mew, mew, I can see you,
Ma, ma, I can see far,
Me, me, I can see some tea.

And they came down and began to peck up the wheat seeds.
But soon it began to get dark and the gulls flew back to their homes on the cliffs
by the sea . . .

Mew, mew, I can see you,
Ma, ma, I can see far,
Me, me, we've had our tea.

In the morning, the farmer gives a big stretch – ah.
Good morning everyone!
After he has eaten a lovely bowl of porridge – mm,
He puts on his boots, one for stumper and one for jumper,
And he calls all the children to help him . . .
He fetches the big wooden rake from its peg in the barn,
And now we are ready to go to the field.

On a Tuesday morning, a sunny Tuesday morning,
We raked our field, Father and I,
We raked it when the sun was high,
We raked our field, Father and I,
We raked it when the sun was high,

Now the birds won't come and peck up the seeds.
And the farmer is so happy he begins to dance and sing with his friends . . .

Song and dance

Oats and beans and barley grow,
Oats and beans and barley grow,
Not you, nor I, nor anyone knows,
How oats and beans and barley grows.

First the farmer sows his seed,
Then he stands and takes his ease,
He stamps his feet and claps his hands,
And turns around to view the land.

However, someone very small came and found that last handful of seed that he
had tipped out under the bramble bush . . .

Poem with actions

A little mouse is gathering, around about she goes,
With twitching ears and whiskers, a sniffling, snuffling nose,
A sniffling snuffling nose.

She has three little children inside her little house,
She needs to go a foraging, that busy little mouse,
That busy little mouse.

She gathers nuts and berries, and little ears of corn,
And softest drifts of Old Man's Beard, to keep her family warm,
To keep her family warm.

So if you see her preening, don't frighten her away,
Just leave a rosy apple and softly creep away,
And softly creep away.

Let us form a ring Dancing as we sing, ring-a-ring-a-rei-a,

Ring-a-ring-a-rei-a, Now we can all turn a-round,

Watch the birds fly up and down, kick-er-i kick-er-i kee!

Our boots are made of lea-ther, Our stock-ings are made of silk, our pin-a-fores are

cal-i-co, as whilte as a-ny milk. Here we go a-round, a-round, a-round, a-

round, a-round, a round. Here we go a-

round, a-round, a-round, un-til we touch the ground.

On a Mon-day morn-ing, a sun-ny Mon-day morn-ing, We sowed our field fa-ther and I,

sowed it when the sun was high, We sowed our field fa-

ther and I, sowed it when the sun was high.

Mew, mew, I can see you. Ma, ma,

I can see far. Mee, mee, I can see some tea.

Oats and beans and bar-ley grow, Oats and beans and bar-ley grow, Not

you not I nor any-one knows, how oats and beans and bar-ley grow.

References for ring-time material

'Let Us Form a Ring' and 'On a Monday Morning' are from N. Foster (ed.), (1985) *Let Us Form a Ring* (Silver Spring, Md.: Acorn Hill Waldorf Kindergarten and Nursery), pp. 31 and 4. 'Oats and Beans' is a traditional game available in H. Wiseman and S. Northcote (undated) *The Clarendon Books of Singing Games: Book 1* (London: Oxford University Press), p. 32. 'Our Boots Are Made of Leather' is a traditional game available in Iona Opie and Peter Opie (1985) *The Singing Game* (London: Oxford University Press). 'A Little Mouse' is an original poem by Lynda Morgan. Other material is by Jill Tina Taplin.

Appendix IV
An example of a child-observation schema

Physical appearance

- What is the size of body, head, limbs and of the parts of the face?
- What are the proportions of body, head, limbs and of the parts of the face?
- What is the skin tone and texture?
- How would you describe the hands, hair, ears?
- What kind of gaze does the child have?

Movement

- How would you describe the child's movements? Flowing, wooden, powerful, hesitant, clumsy, etc.
- How would you describe the child's walk?
- How does the child use tools?
- How does the child imitate movement?
- How does the child eat?

Speech

- How would you describe the child's speech?
- Are there speech defects?
- Where is the centre of speech in the child?
- How does the child most typically express himself or herself? Speech, facial expressions, actions, etc.?

Thinking

How would you characterise the child's

- way of thinking?
- memory?
- ability to learn?
- practical intelligence?

Feeling

What are the child's

- typical ways of expressing himself or herself?
- social faculties and effect on other children?
- likes, dislikes and enthusiasms?
- abilities to change?

Will

- How does the child achieve what he or she wants?
- How would you characterise the child's powers of concentration?
- How would you characterise the child's powers of perseverance?

Keys texts and resources

Alexander, R. (ed.) (2010) *Children, Their World, Their Education: Final Report and Recommendations of the Cambridge Primary Review*, London: Routledge.

Baldwin, Dancy R. (2004) *You Are Your Child's First Teacher*, Stroud: Hawthorn Press. An overview of the Steiner Waldorf picture of the young child and the care that he or she needs.

Carey, D. and Large, J. (2001) *Festivals, Family and Food*, Stroud: Hawthorn Press. A resource book for families based on seasonal celebrations.

Clouder, C. and Nicol, J. (2007) *Creative Play for Your Baby*, London: Gaia Books. Simple toy-making for young children with an overview of child development.

—— (2008) *Creative Play for Your Toddler*, London: Gaia Books. Simple toy-making for young children with an overview of child development.

Druitt, A., Fynes-Clinton, C. and Rowling, M. (1995) *All Year Round*, Stroud: Hawthorn Press. Another seasonal resource book for families.

Drummond, M.-J., Jenkinson, S. and the Steiner Early Years Research Group (2009) 'Meeting the Child: Approaches to Observation and Assessment in Steiner Kindergartens', Faculty of Education, University of Plymouth.

Glockler, M. and Goebel, A. (2007) *Guide to Child Health*, Edinburgh: Floris Press. A complete guide for parents and carers.

Goddard-Blythe, S. (2008) *What Babies and Children Really Need*, Stroud: Hawthorn Press and Alliance for Childhood. Cornerstones of pre-conceptual, pre-natal and early childhood care by the Director of the Institute for Neuro-Psychological Psychology.

Jaffke F. (2002) *Play and Work in Early Childhood*, Edinburgh: Floris Press. An introduction to the Steiner Waldorf picture of child development and teaching methodology enhanced by photographs of settings in action.

—— (2002) *Toymaking with Children*, Edinburgh: Floris Press. A guide to the toys and equipment of a Steiner Waldorf setting and how to make them.

Jenkinson, S. (2002) *The Genius of Play*, Edinburgh: Hawthorn Press. An overview of the importance of play in child development by an experienced Steiner pedagogue.

Jenkinson, S., and Rawson, M. (1998) *Educational Tasks of the Waldorf Curriculum*, Forest Row: SWSF Publications. An overview of the complete Steiner Waldorf school curriculum from kindergarten to school-leaving age.

Lissau, R. (1987) *Rudolf Steiner: His Life, Work, Inner Path and Social Initiatives*, Stroud: Hawthorn Press. An introduction to the initiator of Steiner Waldorf education which includes a broad view of the many areas of his work outside education.

Male, D. (2005) *The Parent and Child Group Handbook: A Steiner/Waldorf Approach*, Stroud: Hawthorn Press. A guide to Steiner Waldorf work in parent-and-child groups.

Nicol, J. (2010) *Bringing the Steiner Waldorf Approach to Your Early Years Practice*, 2nd edn, London: Routledge. An overview of the key principles and practices of the Steiner Waldorf early childhood setting.

Oldfield, L. (2002) *Free to Learn*, Stroud: Hawthorn Press. A detailed picture of the environment and principles of the Steiner Waldorf kindergarten, including international examples, by an experienced Steiner Waldorf kindergarten practitioner.

Patzlaff, R. and Sassmannshausen, W. (eds.) (2007) *Developmental Signatures: Core Values and Practices in Waldorf Education for Children 3–9*, New York: AWSNA. Principles and guidelines for the Steiner Waldorf approach through kindergarten and into school.

Perrow, S. (2008) *Healing Stories for Challenging Behaviour*, Stroud: Hawthorn Press. An introduction to therapeutic story-making.

Schweizer, S. (2007) *Well, I Wonder*, London: Rudolf Steiner Press. An experienced Steiner Waldorf kindergarten practitioner gives examples and guidelines for parents, carers and educators of young children.

—— (2009) *Under the Sky*, London: Rudolf Steiner Press. An experienced Steiner Waldorf kindergarten practitioner gives examples and guidelines for outdoor life for parents, carers and educators of young children.

Steiner, R. (1996) *The Child's Changing Consciousness*, Hudson, NY: Anthroposophic Press. A series of lectures on education given in 1923, after the opening of the first Steiner Waldorf school. The first four are of particular relevance to early childhood work.

—— (1996) *The Education of the Child*, Hudson, NY: Anthroposophic Press. An introductory essay written in 1909 on education from birth to the age of twenty-one.

Suggate, S. P. (2009) 'School Entry Age and Reading Achievement in the 2006 Programme for International Student Assessment (PISA)', *International Journal of Educational Research*, 48: 151–61.

Collections and anthologies

Songs, stories, poems, verses, fairytales, birthdays, etc.

Autumn, Edinburgh: Floris Press. Seasonal Crafts Series.
Autumn, Stroud: Wynstones Press.
Christmas, Edinburgh: Floris Press. Seasonal Crafts Series.
Dancing as We Sing, New York: WECAN Press.
Easter, Edinburgh: Floris Press. Seasonal Crafts Series.
Gateways, Stroud: Wynstones Press.
Let Us Form a Ring, New York: WECAN Press.

Nature, Edinburgh: Floris Press.
The Nature Corner, Edinburgh: Floris Press. Seasonal Crafts Series.
Spindrift, Stroud: Wynstones Press.
Spring, Edinburgh: Floris Press. Seasonal Crafts Series.
Spring, Stroud: Wynstones Press.
Summer, Edinburgh: Floris Press. Seasonal Crafts Series.
Summer, Stroud: Wynstones Press.
Winter, Edinburgh: Floris Press. Seasonal Crafts Series.
Winter, Stroud: Wynstones Press.

Journals and compilations

Kindling: Journal for Steiner Early Childhood Education and Care. (U.K.)
   (Email: earlyyearsnews@aol.com)
An Overview of the Waldorf Kindergarten, 2 vols., New York: WECAN Press.
A Deeper Understanding of the Waldorf Kindergarten, New York: WECAN Press.
The Young Child in the World Today, New York: WECAN Press.

Useful websites

www.steinerwaldorf.org.uk
www.waldorfanswers.org
www.waldorflibrary.org

Resources for craft materials, toys, healthcare and Waldorf equipment

Mecurius, 6 Highfield, Kings Langley WD4 9JT. Tel.: 01923 261 646.
   Website: www.mercurius-international.com
Weleda (UK) Ltd, Heanor Road, Ilkeston DE7 8DR. Tel.: 0115 9448200.
   Website: www.weleda.co.uk.
Myriad Natural Toys, Ringwood, Hampshire. Tel.: 01725 517085.
   Website: www.myriadonline.co.uk and www.waldorf-toys.com.

Index